KEN VALLEDY & EAMONN CAREY

The Startup Lexicon

SECOND EDITION

Demystifying the everyday
language of startups

The Startup Lexicon
Second edition
ISBN 978-1-915483-60-7 (paperback)
ISBN 978-1-915483-61-4 (ebook)

Published in 2024 by Right Book Press
Printed in the UK

A CIP record of this book is available from the British Library.

Lexicon

A list of words commonly used in a particular language, area of interest or profession.

Foreword

Every year, investors see thousands of pitch decks, meet a similar number of founders and dozens of investments. Still, we're only seeing a single grain of sand on a miles-long beach of ideas that people come up with around the world every year. Only a tiny number of those will go on to become successful businesses. The deck is stacked against founders a lot of the time.

This book is a helping hand for people who want to start or join companies, bring a startup mindset into their own business or place of work, or who want to just learn more about the language that's bizarre to most, but in everyday usage in the technology world.

The quote 'fail to prepare, prepare to fail' is often attributed to Ben Franklin, and it's every bit as true today as it was hundreds of years ago. It's a line that a lot of the aspiring founders, operators and even investors I meet could do with considering. So many of them are going into an interview or fundraising process where a substantial chunk of what they hear will be acronyms, technical terms and phrases. The challenge they face is the expectation that they'll be fully conversant in CAC/LTV or the risks of liquidation preferences.

There are online resources that can help with this – some are too detailed, many not enough. The critical thing that Ken Valledy and Eamonn Carey have achieved with this book is bringing simple definitions and real-world stories to make the occasionally impenetrable world of technology language more accessible to anyone who's interested.

Increasingly these words and phrases impact everyday life. When the first edition of this book came out, ChatGPT didn't exist. Generative AI wasn't a phrase that appeared in the press every day. The technology industry moves quickly. The language around it evolves at a similar pace. That's why this second edition is so critical.

Tom Eisenmann, Professor of Business Administration at Harvard Business School, wrote about the andon cord in the Foreword to the first edition of this book. It's a cord that employees on the production line at Toyota can pull when they need help. It stops the line and brings supervisors and quality control people over to the line. I loved that analogy.

Since the first book came out, the concept of an AI copilot is one that we're seeing more and more often. Github has a copilot to help you when you're programming. Google has one in every email, document and beyond – helping you to write, edit, transcribe and more. This is a founder's copilot. Whether you're studying entrepreneurship, starting a company or just interested in learning more about the startup and technology world, it will be a guide, a safety blanket and so much more.

Good luck!

Jenny Fielding
Founder, The Fund

Introduction

Back in July 2022, I was on the banks of the Thames, sipping a cold beer in the summer sunshine, having just attended the launch event for the first edition of *The Startup Lexicon*. Eamonn and I had just been interviewed and we were appreciating this unique moment in time. Our conversation focused on the journey we'd been on together, how the idea for the book had come about and how it felt to be an author. There may have been the odd remark about a second edition, which Eamonn and I agreed was a distinct possibility, but that was it for the time being. However, things changed over the months to come.

Since the launch, the feedback we've had has been truly incredible. The book has found its way to many grateful recipients, from founders and corporate leaders to university professors and students studying entrepreneurship. We were even shortlisted for the Business Book of the Year Award! However, as we spent our time promoting the book, we quickly realised that the language (lexicon) of startups had moved on, and day by day, month by month, more 'new' words (especially in the area of AI) were entering the daily vernacular of the startup world. As a result, we saw that there was already a need to update the book. What seemed like something that was a long way off in the summer of 2022 was a definite 'here and now' subject for discussion in early 2023.

Thankfully, Eamonn was keen to re-form the partnership and we jumped back on the horse and began to flesh out what new definitions and stories should be considered for this new, second edition. The process was the same as before: to agree on which new words should be included, create the definitions and then identify people we felt would be able to provide their own unique stories about many of those words. Many meetings and Zoom/Teams calls later, we're ready to share this new, updated version.

I hope you enjoy this as much as Eamonn and I have enjoyed writing it, and if you do bump into us, please ask us about the third edition, as I have a strange feeling that we'll be contemplating this before long! As they say, watch this space. Stranger things have happened!

Ken Valledy, March 2024

I've always loved words. As a kid, I was the one with my nose buried in a book as I walked along the road to school. That continued into later life when I studied journalism, wrote for magazines, papers and websites, and sent absurdly long emails. Alongside reading, my other passion in life was technology. I was given a Sinclair ZX Spectrum computer in the mid-1980s, and that gift from my parents (which I think my dad secretly had his eye on as a plaything) was the start of a lifelong love of coding, computing and more. The Spectrum's incredible 48K of RAM was my catalyst for experimentation on Ataris, Amigas, PCs, 14.4KB dial-up, broadband, websites, social media, mobile and more. My passion for technology has helped me to start companies, meet some of the best friends and colleagues I've ever had, and given me more opportunities than the six-year-old version of me could ever have imagined.

The combination of tech and words is a fascinating one. From the simplicity of the BASIC programming language to LLMs and beyond, the tech we use and the language we use to describe it has changed at an exponential pace over the course of my life. One of the great things about the tech and investing world in which I now find myself is the constant opportunity to read interesting things, meet amazing people who are working on world-changing ideas and learn more about the technologies that will shape the next ten to twenty years and beyond. It all changes so often that I find myself talking to founders about words, acronyms or slang that are commonplace for many, but confusing for those who are interested in becoming better educated about the industry.

Funnily enough, the first conversation I had with Ken about the first edition of this book happened the morning after one with a founder, who had asked why there wasn't a glossary of terms to help people going through the investment process for the first time. There's plenty of information out there, but it's frequently missing some key words, facts and context. That's what the first edition of this book delivered, and this updated version will hopefully flesh things out even more.

I've been on an incredible journey since the first edition of *The Startup Lexicon* came out. I've delivered talks, lectures, Q&A sessions and more across Europe, Asia and the US, and have seen copies of the book spread out around the world. The level of passion, engagement, enthusiasm and interest people have in the tech industry is incredible to witness, and also understandable, given the impact that tech is having and will continue to have on all our lives.

Hopefully, as you go through your journey as a student, teacher, interested observer, founder, team member or anyone else in the industry, this book will prove to be a valuable resource. Given how quickly the language in this sector evolves, I suspect version three will be with you before too long, so please forgive any omissions, enjoy the definitions and the stories, and feel free to contact me on X @eamonncarey to let me know what you'd like to see more or less of in the next edition.

Eamonn Carey, March 2024

How to use this book

The Startup Lexicon contains 278 short definitions of terms that are used in the startup, tech and investing worlds – and occasionally beyond. It's designed to give you an inch-deep, mile-wide understanding of some of the words and phrases that are commonplace in those industries. To liven things up a little, we also asked some of our friends to contribute anecdotes, stories and their own thoughts on some of the definitions that we felt needed to be fleshed out in more detail. As you work your way through the definitions, you may find terms, phrases, acronyms or abbreviations that you haven't come across before. The goal of this book is to help you learn as much as possible about this evolving language, so keep checking through the alphabetical list to cross-reference the terms that are new to you. For example, the definition of VC appears towards the end of the book, but we reference it frequently earlier on. You can be sure that, if we've mentioned a specific term, there will be a definition of it somewhere in the book.

A/B testing

Also known as split testing, this is an experiment conducted by companies. They show two or more variants of a web page or app that has a specific conversion goal (ie getting people to click download, get started, sign up now or take another action) to users at random. The results of the test are then collated to determine which version has the best outcome or conversion rate. Perhaps one of the most famous examples of this was when Google tested 41 shades of blue to determine the optimal shade for their logo.

Accelerator

A programme (also known as an accelerator programme) that allows startups to join a group or cohort of other companies for a fixed period of time, usually between three and six months, conducted in person or virtually. Most accelerators provide access to capital, educational programming, mentorship and a network of partners, investors and other companies. Y Combinator, Techstars, 500 Startups and OnDeck are among the best-known accelerator programmes globally, but there are hundreds of others run by organisations, universities, municipalities and other bodies. Most accelerators take between 6 and 8 per cent of the equity in a company in exchange for an investment of between $100 and $150,000. Companies such as Airbnb, Dropbox, Stripe, Digital Ocean, Coinbase and Reddit are all accelerator alumni.

Accredited investor

There are several categories of accredited investor, but the term generally refers to high net worth individuals (HNWIs), banks, investment funds and corporate entities permitted to invest in securities that aren't registered with the Securities and Exchange Commission in the United States. Most startup and scaleup businesses meet these criteria. For example, to qualify as an accredited investor in the United States, an individual must have a net worth of at least $1 million or an annual salary of $200,000 or above. The rules around accredited investors vary from country to country, and in many cases are being reviewed due to the rise of crowdfunding platforms and other tools that allow individuals to invest in these unregistered securities.

Acqui-hiring

When a company decides to acquire another company purely to recruit its employees rather than to own its products or services. In general, these transactions don't result in a return to the company's investors, but instead involve employees receiving equity or options in the acquiring company.

Add-on service

An additional feature, product or service that companies sell alongside their primary product. For example, a B2B company may offer a SaaS product, but also have an implementation package or option that customers can purchase for an additional cost. For example, many artificial intelligence (AI) machine learning (ML) companies sell a product where the primary revenue stream is a SaaS product, but an installation and training package is necessary for companies to understand and make the best use of the product.

Agile

A project management methodology that has its origins in the 2001 Agile Manifesto, which details four values and twelve principles for Agile software development. The methodology breaks up a project into multiple phases. Often used in software development, it allows for iteration and changes in the product spec. It demands an extremely high degree of collaboration between the various stakeholders involved in the process. Agile teams tend to work in two- to four-week sprints, meeting regularly to review the results and iterate according to any updates or requirements.

> *Ah... Agile: a word that has been so bastardised within some large organisations over the past few years. But what is it and why is it important? In essence, Agile is an iterative approach to project management and software development that helps teams to deliver value to their customers faster and with fewer issues. This promise is driven by a belief that, instead of betting everything on a 'big bang' launch (sometimes referred to as waterfall project management, where you only start a new phase when the previous one is complete), an Agile team delivers work in small but consumable increments.*

Requirements, plans and results are continuously evaluated, which means that teams have a natural mechanism for responding to change without having to wait for a formalised monthly check-in or update. If something needs to be updated or changed, in principle it can happen faster using an Agile approach rather than a waterfall one.

What I have come to appreciate is that Agile is based on several values:

1. *individuals and interactions over processes and tools*
2. *working software over comprehensive documentation*
3. *customer collaboration over contract negotiation*
4. *responding to change over following a plan.*

Although Agile is closely linked with software development, its principles can be applied to many projects. When it's adopted by large organisations, it's important that they don't confuse speed with doing the right thing. Yes, it's crucial to move quickly but, no matter how fast you move, it's garbage in, garbage out. Remember that the customer pays your wages and you need to focus on delivering value for them and being responsive to their ever-evolving needs and desires. Please remember that Agile is just an approach and doesn't guarantee success. In order for the approach to work, you need to ensure that the entire organisation gets it and is set up to succeed.

Mick Doran, *research consultant, NatWest; co-founder, Noggin the Brain People*

Agile software development

See above.

AI prompt

A question, statement or command that a user inputs into an AI model to initiate an action or response. The prompt usually serves as the starting point for the AI model's generation process, guiding it towards generating content that's relevant to whatever you're asking for. The quality of the prompt can greatly affect the quality of the output generated by the AI model.

Alpha testing

This is usually the first phase of software testing that businesses will engage in. Alpha testing is conducted to receive feedback, either in-house or with a limited subset of friends, family, connections or investors. Companies iterate on their product after the alpha stage before moving onto a beta release, which goes out to a wider pool of users or customers.

Angel Capital Association

The professional association of active accredited investors in North America. In the UK, the equivalent body is the UKBAA (UK Business Angels Association).

Angel investor

A high net worth individual who provides financial backing for startups or entrepreneurs, usually in exchange for equity in the company. Angel investors can sometimes be found within an entrepreneur's network of family and friends, but are more likely to be successful founders, operators or business people. Groups of angel investors sometimes band together to co-invest in a syndicate.

Angel investing is what got me into this whole world. I was fortunate enough to have some success in business, and a huge portion of that can be attributed to the knowledge, guidance and expertise of folks who took time to have coffee or a beer with me almost 20 years ago. Every founder stands on the shoulders of others, and having the right people around the table with you is invaluable. Those coffees and beers were foundational moments for me, and fundamental ones in my journey as a founder.

With that in mind, it was incredible to start getting requests for help, support, advice, a shoulder to cry on and more from other founders as my own ventures started to scale. One of the jokes I told founders when I was running accelerator programmes is that we teach them about all the mistakes we've made so that they can avoid them, then go and make a bunch of new mistakes before coming back and teaching them how to avoid those. My view was that if I could help one company avoid the myriad detours and wrong turns along the way, then I'd be paying things forward in the right way.

That decision to spend time with younger startups was the start of my angel investing journey. The more time I spent with founders, the more I started thinking about how I could help, how I could get more involved and how I could stay involved beyond an initial conversation. It didn't hurt that they were all substantially smarter than me, with better ideas to boot – so getting behind them made a lot of sense.

My first angel investment came about after a conversation with a founder who was building a new way for people to work – no more centralised offices, but rather a network of spaces where individuals, teams and whole companies could come together on a full-time or ad hoc basis (or a combo thereof) to work. As someone who'd struggled with leases, office moves and more, this sounded like manna from heaven: someone solving an itch I felt myself.

It grew from there – from backing people who were solving problems that I'd faced myself, or ones that I really understood, to starting to work with people who were solving problems that I thought the world deserved to have solved, or ones that would just make people healthier, happier or better off. Over the past six or seven years of being an angel investor, I've not only been lucky enough to invest in some great companies, I've also had the good fortune to broaden my horizons when it comes to new technologies, new geographies and much more besides. More importantly, I've met some incredible people and made some friends that I'm fortunate enough to be able to support on their ventures.

Angel investing isn't for everyone. There are no guarantees of returns. Everyone hopes for a $50,000 ticket into Uber that turns into £200 million – frankly, I would've taken £500 for £200,000. If you only chase *those types of opportunities, you'll struggle to find them. What's worked for me is to work with smart, driven, passionate, engaging founders who want to change the world. There's a chance they will, and the energy they project will attract others – and if you're a great angel and a solid support, you'll be the first intro they make.*

Eamonn Carey, *general partner, Tera Ventures*

Angel network

Also known as an angel group, this is a collection of angel investors who meet regularly to evaluate and invest in startups. These networks or groups tend to be structured geographically around specific interests or alumni/professional networks. For example, EstBAN is the Estonian Business Angels Network, SpotiAngels is a group of Spotify employees who invest together and Alma Angels is a group focused on investing in female founders.

Annex fund

Also known as a sidecar, continuity or continuation fund, this is an additional side fund that provides an extra pot of money to supplement fund investments. For example, many pre-seed and seed funds have continuity funds that allow them to make larger investments in their portfolio companies at later stages.

Annual recurring revenue (ARR)

This is a key metric used by companies such as SaaS subscription businesses that have subscription agreements. Standard formula: ARR = (overall subscription cost per year + recurring revenue from add-ons or upgrades) – revenue lost from cancellations.

Anthropomorphism

In a general sense, this is the attribution of human traits and emotions to non-human entities. In the context of AI, anthropomorphism is about making machines appear human-like and interact in the same way as humans. For example, the former Microsoft Bing chatbot Sydney and the xAI equivalent Grok have both been given 'human' names and personalities. Likewise, robots such as Boston Dynamics' Spot and Tesla's Optimus are designed to look like a dog and a human respectively rather than looking like purely mechanical robots.

Anti-dilution provision

These are contract clauses that allow investors the right to protect and maintain their current ownership percentages, even if new shares are issued in future investment rounds.

Articles of association (UK) / Articles of incorporation (US)

A set of formal papers filed with a government body to legally document the creation of a corporation/limited company. In the UK, these are known as articles of association. In the US, they're articles of incorporation.

Artificial general intelligence (AGI)

A form of AI that's capable of executing human-level tasks that standard computer systems can't achieve. Today, AI can perform numerous tasks but not at the level that would equate to human intelligence. AGI remains a developing concept but, in the future, examples of AGI applications might include fully autonomous vehicles in which a high level of reasoning and autonomous decision making would be required.

Assets under management (AUM)

A term used in the investment world to indicate the total amount of money or assets under management by entities such as venture capital or hedge funds, wealth management companies or individual portfolio managers.

Artificial intelligence (AI)

This refers to the creation of computer systems that can do things that usually require human intelligence. It's about teaching computers to learn, think, solve problems, understand language and make decisions. In the business world, AI is a game changer because it allows machines to handle tasks that would normally require human brain power.

> *There are two main types of AI: narrow AI and general AI. Narrow AI is like a specialist – it's good at one specific task, such as sorting data or recognising faces. General AI would be more like a generalist, capable of*

handling various tasks and learning from them, almost like a human. AI systems use different approaches. Some follow a set of rules, others learn from data (machine learning) and some mimic the structure of the human brain (neural networks). For example, machine learning helps businesses by analysing data to make predictions or automate processes.

In practical terms, AI is behind things such as virtual assistants, personalised recommendations and even self-driving cars. Businesses are increasingly using AI to improve efficiency, cut costs and make better decisions. However, it's essential to use AI responsibly, taking ethical aspects into consideration and being transparent about how it's being used in business operations.

I think of AI as machines being able to do human thinking/analysis at scale. It started off with machine learning, with AI being able to do lots of calculations very fast. In 2023, we started to see it appear in writing and image creation. One academic told me to think of the latest AI as a monkey with a PhD. And a global partner in a consulting firm told me it's like having five graduates with little life experience at your disposal.

In 2024, we're seeing the equivalent of a creative production team. The mantra is now that AI itself won't take your job but it will be taken by the person who knows how to use AI. Be aware that AI is moving quickly and changing every week, so keep up to date. It's impacting some industry verticals more than others, so take a look. Today we're seeing applications that focus on automation, so now AI is *shifting into performing more complex tasks at scale, the latest being video creation. Full disclosure: I used generative AI to help me shape this definition!*

Vijay Solanki, *VP of brand and communications, Sinorbis*

Artificial neural network (ANN)

A neural network is used in AI to teach computers how to process data in a way that's inspired by the human brain. It's a type of machine learning known as deep learning that uses interconnected nodes (or neurons) in a layered structure that resembles the human brain.

Augmented intelligence

A subset of AI in which artificial intelligence assists humans, rather than looking to replace them for performing tasks. It's typically done using machine learning to analyse data to help humans make smarter decisions. Humans can use augmented intelligence to enhance their existing capabilities and tools. For example, by mining big data for patterns and predictive indicators, online stores can try to predict individual customer preferences.

Average revenue per user (ARPU)

This measures the average amount of revenue generated per user over a given period of time. It's calculated by dividing your total revenue by the number of users using your service. For example, if a SaaS business has 1,000 users and generates £10,000 in monthly recurring revenue, their ARPU would be £10.

ARPU is a really important metric, particularly for consumer-facing businesses as they scale. Most businesses start by growing their user base, but ARPU measures more than just volume growth; it gives an indication of the underlying value of your customer base. As a measure of the value, longevity and sustainability of any business, investors reviewing business plans will primarily look for user growth, but they'll also look for ARPU growth.

ARPU growth can come from increasing the price of your product or by selling a range of products and pushing the mix of products towards those that are of higher value and more expensive.

At Sky, which is fundamentally a subscription model business, we reached a point where we had topped out the number of users/subscribers we could realistically get and pivoted to focus entirely on ARPU growth – selling more products to the same customer and trying to upgrade them to more expensive products. This was a successful strategy and helped build further brand and platform loyalty, but timing was crucial to getting it right. If we'd done it too early we would've hampered the core user growth.

As with any average measure, it has its limitations. If you blend an average of a lot of products at different price points in different markets with different currencies, it can become much less meaningful.

Investors will often use ARPU as a sense check of your pricing vs other competitor products and the market overall, and look for an upward trend. They'll *also compare your ARPU to your retail price (the one that's advertised to users) to see if you're discounting too heavily or if additional costs such as sales tax are hampering your unit economics. ARPU is a critical measure to understand and show improvement in the unit economics of your business, and should be carefully tracked and managed.*

Serena Martin, *ex BBC, Sky and BritBox International; startup mentor and advisor*

B

Basic attention token (BAT)

A blockchain-based system built on Ethereum that's used for tracking media consumers' time and attention on websites, using the Brave web browser. Its goal is to efficiently distribute advertising funds between advertisers, publishers and readers of online content and advertisements.

Beta testing

The final round of testing before a product is launched to a wider audience. Beta testing will often take between four and eight weeks, although Google's Gmail service was famously in beta for five years. Beta testing is where a larger group of users and customers will test the product and provide feedback ahead of a full public release. The purpose is to help companies make any last-minute changes or updates that are necessary before a more formal launch or push.

During my time at Duel (I joined as employee number four back in 2016), we pivoted our product offering three times. This meant that our SaaS product underwent a series of redevelopment and testing phases.

In contrast to alpha testing, which primarily focuses on identifying and fixing previously undiscovered bugs and is usually performed by internal team members, beta testing is all about getting your product into the hands of real clients and end users, allowing them to test it in real-life scenarios. The goal of beta testing is to gather customer feedback on the product and its potential use cases and refine it accordingly, usually involving multiple rounds of testing. It's a crucial phase of product or software development before an official launch.

Additionally, beta testing provides startups with an opportunity to gain insights not just into the product's performance but also into user behaviour, preferences and patterns, which can be looped back to inform the sales and marketing teams.

At Duel, we strategically used beta testing as a way of acquiring our first paid customers. First, we selected a targeted group of brands and SMEs we wanted to partner with, then closely collaborated with them during the test and collected as much data as possible (which can be rather challenging at this stage). Such early involvement in the product iteration and development processes meant that our beta testers felt more invested from the beginning, making it easier for us to retain and convert them into paid customers.

The main piece of advice I have for beta testing is to always be on hand and proactive with your beta testers. Treat it as a collaborative and user-centric approach, allowing you to get closer to your end users, understand them better and uncover any unforeseen product use cases that you or the *development team might not have anticipated. It's an exciting stage of product development!*

Inga Driksne, *operations advisor to early-stage founders*

Bitcoin

A decentralised virtual currency (comparable to an online version of cash) that can be sent from individual to individual via a peer to peer network (P2P), without the involvement of intermediaries. (See also: Blockchain.)

Black swan

A term used to describe a completely unpredictable event. Black swans are by their nature extremely rare but have severe consequences. In his book *The Black Swan: The impact of the highly improbable* (2007), Nicholas Nassim Taleb wrote that the event must be a surprise and have a major impact, but with the benefit of hindsight and data, it becomes rationalised. Examples of black swan events are the dissolution of the Soviet Union, the impact and spread of the World Wide Web, and the Covid-19 pandemic.

Bloatware

This has two distinct but slightly differing meanings. It's primarily used to describe unwanted or even harmful software or applications that are pre-installed on a device. These can frequently take up storage space and slow down device performance. Similarly, it's used to describe software that's excessively complex or has unnecessary features that make it less useful or more difficult to use.

Blockchain

Unlike traditional databases where information is stored on one hard drive or server, a blockchain distributes information across all the computers (or nodes) on that network. This means that, in theory, the information is decentralised, and therefore more private and secure than in a more centralised model where there's a single point of failure. Perhaps the most famous example is the Bitcoin blockchain, where the blockchain ensures the integrity of that currency by encrypting, validating and permanently recording transactions.

> *When people speak of blockchain, they speak of Bitcoin and a chain of blocks connected by the solving of mathematical problems – a process that's now known as 'mining' in the crypto world. There's nothing wrong with those early descriptions, but there are now many, many different kinds of blockchains: some public, some private, and some downright scammy. For public blockchains, the main problem is that everybody can see every transaction.*
>
> *Imagine owing somebody £100, paying that amount into their personal bank account and being able to see not only that transfer, but also every other transaction they've ever made. That creates serious privacy issues and can lead to situations such as front-running, where bad actors can hijack your trade or transfer by paying a higher premium ('gas fee').*
>
> *Moreover, blockchains are evolving. Currently, there's an archipelago of blockchain islands that are gradually becoming connected by virtual ferries, bridges and ramps, thus creating a system*

> *that improves the efficiency and interoperability of blockchains. This is a million miles from the first version of blockchain, but is undoubtedly where blockchain is heading. People keep talking about the metaverse, but I believe the real future is in connected blockchains that enable the metaverse and technologies such as NFTs. Long live blockchain.*

> **Monty Munford**, *co-founder, Home Truth*

Book value

A measure used by investors and others to determine the value of a company. In essence, it equates to the total value of a company's assets (including any equity value) minus its outstanding liabilities.

Bootstrapping

The process of building a company from scratch with nothing but revenue, personal money or savings. A bootstrapped company doesn't have any funding from outside partners or investors.

> *This is a word that will come in useful when starting your own business. I've helped thousands of people turn an idea or passion into a way of making a living, and the crux of my advice for the early days is to maximise sales and minimise costs. Indeed, the way I present this to early-stage founders is to beg, borrow and barter when starting out. Need a kitchen space to start your business? Rent one by the hour as opposed to taking on a year-round commitment.*

Want to host a product launch? Secure free space from someone who would welcome the community you bring into that space and invite brands that want to raise their profile with your audience to cover the catering costs. In the early stages of your business, think about how you can avoid costs by working with an army of supporters and complementary brands that want access to what you have to offer. Everyone loves a startup, particularly large organisations such as big corporates and universities. Get to know them, as they have access to people, space, funding, clients and mentorship. When you're young in business, this equates to access that money simply can't buy. These organisations want to help you succeed – and they'll enable you to bootstrap your way to growth. As you grow, you'll start paying for space, tech, talented people and activities to motivate and retain those talented people. This all costs. But my advice to any founder, at whatever stage of business, is to keep a sharp eye on the figures and retain a bootstrapping state of mind. It will serve you well.

Emma Jones CBE, *founder, Enterprise Nation*

Bridge round

A funding round that happens in between larger funding rounds. Bridge rounds provide a top-up to help companies achieve the goals, metrics and KPIs (key performance indicators) they need to unlock a larger round of funding. Most bridge rounds are funded by existing investors, but sometimes accommodate new ones.

This is a round that happens when you haven't built sufficient proof points to raise the next proper round. It's usually provided by internal investors and should be considered as their support to you and the company. Looking at this definition, it seems that the company hasn't fulfilled its goals and hence feels like a negative.

In such situations, experienced investors often ask, 'Is it a bridge or a pier?' This indicates that the additional runway may still be too short to achieve sufficient milestones to be able to convince investors to invest the next level of money (or any further money). But even if the situation is difficult, the added time allows you to apply entrepreneurial creativity, which can overcome any obstacle. If you have good investors on board, they may even throw you more than one consecutive lifeline. They may have seen that you can eventually deliver good results and build this into their high-conviction approach to investing. It can be highly valuable to have such investors on board, so try to understand the approach and mentality of your investors beforehand and select the right ones.

When you carry out due diligence on your potential investors, you should also investigate this bridge financing aspect and their behaviour in difficult situations in general. A bridge round can happen in a positive situation as well – internal investors may be excited about your developments and especially the outlook. They may give you additional money so that you can raise the next round at better terms than you currently could. It's probably

> *best to try to portray all bridge rounds in such light,*
> *as it boosts the self-confidence of everyone involved.*
> *To be able to do so, the terms of the bridge round*
> *should not be onerous.*
>
> **Andrus Oks**, *founding partner, Tera Ventures*

Broker

Someone who acts on behalf of individuals and companies to help them raise capital. They usually work with a network of funds, high net worth individuals and others to present deals. Brokers will often take a success fee and also equity in companies they help. They usually work with later-stage scaleup businesses, but sometimes work with earlier-stage companies.

Build verification testing

See: Smoke testing.

Burn rate

This is typically expressed in terms of the total amount of money that a company is spending every month, covering all their costs: salaries, offices, overheads and incidentals. Your burn rate is closely related to your runway and cash-out date.

Business to business (B2B)

In the startup world, B2B is used to describe companies that are selling their products or services to other businesses. For example, Intercom is a well-known B2B business that sells its platform to other startups, scaleups and large enterprises.

Business to business to consumer (B2B2C)

Combining the B2B and B2C models, this is a business model where company one (the first B) sells their product or service in partnership with company two (the second B) to an end customer (C). Examples of B2B2C companies or platforms are OpenTable, Resy and other reservation platforms. Restaurants and bars contract with the platform, which enables an end user to make a booking.

Business to consumer (B2C)

B2C companies sell their products directly to their customers. Examples of this include popular language learning applications such as Lingvist and Duolingo, as well as physical products such as Kencko, Allbirds, Ohne and others that sell their smoothies, shoes and menstrual cycle products respectively directly to the consumer. (See also: DTC.)

Buyout

A type of merger and acquisition (M&A), this is a transaction where a company (or investor) acquires a controlling interest or 100 per cent ownership of another company. Examples of buyout M&A deals include Facebook's acquisitions of WhatsApp and Instagram.

Cap

Short for valuation cap. Typically found in a simple agreement for safe equity (SAFE) or convertible notes, a valuation cap allows investors to see their investment converted into equity at a set maximum price. For example, if a company raises capital from investors on a SAFE or convertible note with a cap of £5 million, but raises the next round at an £8 million valuation, the SAFE/note investor would see their investment convert into equity at the £5 million valuation cap.

Capital

A generic term that includes anything that delivers value or benefit to its owner, eg equipment, warehouse, intellectual property (IP). Capital can also include cash that's being put to work for productive or investment purposes.

Capital call

A term used in the venture capital or private equity industry. It refers to the call for investment capital made by venture capital funds when they're investing in a new deal or calling for management fees or expenses. VC funds talk about their fund size, but in practice they don't have that capital resting in their bank account. Instead, they draw down or call capital on a deal-by-deal and/or quarterly/biannual/annual basis. When a fund commits to making an investment, they then issue a capital call to their LPs (see: Limited partner), who send their share of the investment to the fund, which then uses that capital to make their investment.

Capital expenditure

Also known as CapEx, these are funds used by a company to purchase, upgrade and maintain physical assets that may include property, plants, buildings, technology or equipment.

Capital under management

See: Assets under management.

Capitalisation table

Also known as cap table, this provides an analysis of a company's percentages of ownership, equity dilution and value of equity at each round of investment by founders, investors and other owners. Cap tables become increasingly important as companies grow, as investors prefer founders and teams to retain sufficient equity ownership to remain incentivised.

Capitalise

A company is able to capitalise by raising capital, usually in exchange for equity or in the form of debt. That capital will then be used to fund the ongoing expenses of the business.

Carried interest

Also known as carry, this is a term used to describe the share of profits that investors receive as compensation in the event of a successful fund or individual investment outcome. Investment funds commonly charge between 0 and 30 per cent carry on the profits they make, with 20 per cent being the standard. For example, if a fund has £100 million AUM and they return £200 million to their investors, the carry applies to the profits generated. In this instance the carry would be 20 per cent of £100 million, which amounts to £20 million in carry. This is then split at an agreed rate between the investment team members.

Cash flow positive

Accountant-speak that means more money is coming in than going out. This is when, after deducting your expenses from your earnings, you still have a positive amount in your bank account. It's also referred to as 'staying in the black' and is especially important when you're self-funded.

Cash-out date

This provides a rough estimate of when a business will run out of cash. It's a metric that's usually expressed as the number of months before the cash runs out. In most cases, this metric is used by companies that aren't yet profitable. For example, a company burning £50,000 per month with £500,000 in the bank will have a cash-out date of ten months. (See also: Runway.)

Central bank digital currency (CBDC)

A CBDC is a digital form of a country's currency issued by that country's central bank, which gives it the same legal status as traditional cash. It's denominated in the national currency (GBP/USD, etc) and can be used to make different types of payments. It's important to note that a CBDC is not cryptocurrency. The connection to the central bank means it's not decentralised.

Churn rate

The annual percentage rate at which customers stop subscribing to a service or employees leave a job.

> *Churn rate is an important metric for any potential investor or corporate assessing a potential partnership with a startup. This revealing percentage often demonstrates the perceived value of the product or service in the eye of the consumer, and thus is a reliable indicator when trying to determine business value. Plenty of factors can affect churn rate: price, product performance, service level and customer satisfaction, to name just a few. It ultimately gives a good insight into the lifetime value and long-term health of the business.*
>
> *Churn rates are incredibly important for subscription services. While working at a general insurance company, we looked at a potential partnership with a telematics provider that was offering affordable car insurance for younger adults. Car-based telematics is a type of 'black box' technology that continuously monitors your driving performance. If*

your performance falls within certain measurements, you pay less on your insurance. In effect, you're rewarded for driving sensibly, the bonus being that the insurance is provided on a rolling monthly contract, meaning there's no long-term commitment. The provider had a great proposition but unfortunately the technology often gave customers inaccurate driving scores. It failed to meet customer expectations and the churn rate of customers dropping the insurance was high at three months. It was a classic example of the churn rate being a strong indicator that it wasn't a suitable partnership to pursue at that time.

Jim Edwards, *digital innovation lead EMEA, Kimberly-Clark*

ChatGPT

An advanced system created by OpenAI that uses a large language model to power a chatbot that engages with users in a way that feels natural and almost human-like. Since the launch of ChatGPT, several other companies have launched similar systems. Google launched Bard (now Gemini), Anthropic launched Claude and Mistral launched le chat, for example.

ChatGPT began as an innovative form of AI designed to converse naturally, learning from extensive human interactions, texts and vast information databases. Initially capable of simple chats and generating jokes, over time it steadily evolved into a sophisticated conversationalist.

Its development marked a significant shift in

AI technology. Initially, it helped businesses by providing efficient customer service solutions and helped students to learn through personalised educational support. Its adaptive nature allowed it to delve into complex subjects, even assisting medical professionals in exploring diverse medical queries.

The widespread adoption of ChatGPT stemmed not only from its practical utility but also from its ability to establish genuine connections with users. As it honed its conversational skills, it adapted to different communication styles and earned the trust of its users, becoming more than just a tool but also a reliable companion in conversations. However, its usefulness also posed challenges. Eliminating hallucinations [see: Hallucination], ensuring accuracy, maintaining user privacy and upholding fairness in interactions became essential priorities.

Over time, ChatGPT expanded its applications to various sectors. It assisted legal professionals in sifting through vast amounts of legal data, supported engineers in problem solving and aided marketers in understanding consumer behaviour through data analysis. Moreover, it played a role in mental health support by providing empathetic conversations to those in need, and it even facilitated creative writing by generating prompts and ideas.

As time went by, ChatGPT transformed into a symbol of how sophisticated technology blended with human-like conversational skills, fundamentally altering the landscape of communication and learning.

Daniel Sawko*, *co-founder shipshape.vc (* AI prompter, not author)*

Clawback

A type of clause that's inserted into some startups' employment agreements to allow the companies to claw back any stock options from the employee if, for example, they leave early, underperform or are a bad leaver (a broad term that covers everything from being fired for causing damage to the company, bringing the company into disrepute or otherwise being removed). In essence, this means that the company can force their employees to forfeit or sell their shares back to it.

Climate tech

This refers to a broad range of innovative solutions aimed at mitigating and adapting to the impacts of climate change. Examples of sectors within climate tech include electric vehicles, green hydrogen and carbon capture and storage. These sectors provide solutions to reduce greenhouse gas emissions, increase energy efficiency and promote a more sustainable use of the planet's resources.

Cockroach

A somewhat pejorative way of describing a startup or company that grows slowly and steadily, with a greater focus on revenue and profitability rather than hyper scaling. People also talk about companies going into 'cockroach mode', which means they scale back operations to focus on staying alive, sustainability and incremental growth.

Cohort

A group of people who share something in common (eg a startup accelerator cohort of startup companies).

> *The relationships you build during a cohort can be game changers for your business.*
>
> *Something magical happens when you put a group of people together on an intense 12-week programme. There's this amazing sense of community and belonging that sticks around long after the programme ends. In my experience at BlockDojo, each cohort connects with each other so well that it's like having a squad of peers who've got your back through all the highs and lows of entrepreneurship. Everyone attends workshops, presentations and 1-2-1s, plus there are always mentors on hand to help you grow. I think it's all about meaningful connections, shared experiences and, above all, camaraderie.*
>
> **Jan McGinley**, *community director, BlockDojo*

Committed capital

The money an investor agrees to contribute to a venture capital or other investment fund. Typically, VC funds don't require their limited partners to fund their entire commitment upfront. Instead, the committed capital is drawn down on a deal-by-deal basis or pre-agreed schedule.

Common stock

A term used to denote shares of ownership in a company. The most common form of share ownership is common stock (shares), which is the class of shares that most early-stage investors and employees will earn. Common stockholders also have voting rights in the company, but are last in line for a return in the event of an exit, with creditors and preferred shareholders receiving the share of any capital returned first.

Community

Also known as ecosystem, this term is used to denote multiple types of groups. A community can be location based – people frequently refer to the San Francisco ecosystem or community. It can be sector specific – eg the fintech community in London. It can also be used in conjunction with accelerator programmes, as well as online/offline groups that support the various stake-holders involved in a community.

> *'If you want to go fast, go alone. If you want to go far, go together.' – African proverb.*
>
> *Building a startup in isolation is self-defeating. To succeed, founders need help from a disparate set of resource providers, including insights from customers, capital from investors, talent from labour pools, knowledge from experienced entrepreneurs and connections from mentors, to name a few. They also need emotional and social support to endure the hard road ahead.*
>
> *That's why startup communities are so valuable.*

> *A startup community exists for one purpose: to help entrepreneurs succeed. These networks of deep human relationships are composed of people who – through their interactions, attitudes, interests, goals, sense of purpose, shared identity, fellowship, collective accountability and stewardship of place – are committed to the positive-sum game of entrepreneurial vibrancy in their community.*
>
> *Not only can a startup community help you build your business, but it can also help you live a more balanced and enjoyable life.*
>
> **Ian Hathaway**, *co-founder and general partner, Far Out Ventures; co-author,* The Startup Community Way

Composable

Composability is one of the core concepts of DeFi. Part of the magic of decentralised finance on Ethereum is that the protocols running on top of the network can be used interchangeably with one another, allowing users to put their assets to work in a variety of ways via smart contracts. In other words, they are composable – interchangeable 'LEGO-like' building blocks that can be added, erased and reorganised as required.

Consensus mechanism

A program used in blockchain systems to attain distributed agreement about a ledger's state. It's usually applied in a network with numerous processes and users. Distributed ledgers, cryptocurrencies and blockchains benefit from their application, as a consensus mechanism replaces much slower human auditing and verifiers.

Confidence testing

See: Smoke testing.

Conversion rate

A variable KPI that tracks the conversion of users/ customers from one stage in their user journey to a more advanced stage. For example, ecommerce websites track the conversion from site visits to purchases and consumer mobile apps track conversion from download to registration, registration to engaged user, registration to paying user, and so on.

Convertible note

This is a popular method through which companies can raise capital from investors. It's an investment agreement that's a form of short-term debt, which converts into equity in a subsequent funding round. Like most debt, it's subject to interest, but rather than getting money back with interest, that investment converts into a slightly larger equity stake in the company. Convertible notes are usually structured with a valuation cap or a discount, which will have an impact on precisely how much equity the investor will receive at that next round of funding.

A convertible note is usually used at the pre-seed and sometimes seed stage rounds of funding. The main distinction from a straight equity investment is that it doesn't initially have a fixed valuation. Instead, it's tied to the valuation of the next round (usually at a discount; there's an interest component as well, which makes

*these notes attractive to investors). Besides the fact
that it makes the negotiation easier (you don't need to
agree on a specific valuation, just the discount), it's also
a simpler contract, so the transaction cost and legal fees
are lower and the deal can close faster.*

*Some investors treat convertible notes as a lottery
ticket or exploratory investment – it's useful for them
to learn about the company ahead of a future round
of funding, but it's not yet a firm commitment. This is
especially true in the case of so-called 'party rounds',
when many investors invest using convertible notes and
nobody has a controlling interest or dominant position.
In some of these cases, it may be that a straight
equity structure and proper lead investor position
would compel the investor to take the company more
seriously. With these notes, it's advisable to set an upper
and lower boundary to the conversion – a valuation cap
and a floor. The valuation cap sets an upper limit that
reduces the misalignment between the parties, and the
valuation floor makes sure that in negative scenarios
or at the maturity date of the loan the dilution would
not be too steep. The loan could either be converted
automatically at the maturity date or investors could ask
for repayment – which is a difficult scenario for most
early-stage companies.*

*In case several investors have invested using
a note, companies should also think about how to
handle the right to convert vs asking for repayment.
For instance, if the lead investor has the right to
decide and others need to follow, you can avoid
some messy scenarios with individual decisions.*

Alongside pre-seed and seed rounds, convertible

notes are the main instruments used in bridge rounds. This is useful because internal investors usually prefer not to set a new valuation as well as avoid using the previous one, which can cause undesirable dilution and a negative signal for the company. In this scenario, valuation cap and floor are not usually used. This also avoids creating a negative signal to new investors.

Some people prefer the straight equity deal because it's a better alignment of interest between the founders (and the previous shareholders) and the new investor. Essentially, the investor who has invested in the convertible note has an incentive not to maximise the valuation of the company – if the note converts at a lower valuation, then the investor gets a larger shareholding. If you want your investors to add value, you should try to motivate them to do so as well, and in general you should make sure that all parties are properly aligned.

Andrus Oks, *founding partner, Tera Ventures*

Convertible preferred stock

A special class of stock issued by a company that allows the owner the right to convert to a fixed number of common stock shares after a predetermined timespan.

Corporate venture capital (CVC)

The investment of a corporation's funds directly into external startup companies. The main objective of CVC is to gain a competitive advantage and access to new, innovative companies and technologies.

One of the most insightful observations I've heard about corporate venture capital, which I quote in my book on corporate startup partnering, Gorillas Can Dance, *was made by Silicon Valley Bank's Gerald Brady: 'A corporation can partner [with a startup] without investing, but it can't invest without partnering.' Arguably, even before large corporations established startup partner programmes (eg BMW StartupGarage), they had established venture capital arms (eg BMW's iVentures). CVC investments are not merely (or primarily) about financial return; they can also be strategic considerations such as gaining a window on new technologies or influence over a key exchange partner. Brady's observation suggests that, if these benefits are to be realised, it's vital for the investing corporation to treat its investee startups as genuine partners.*

Not everyone is convinced about the value of CVC. Some think that what startups primarily need from corporations is their custom, not investment (for which they can turn to traditional VCs) – thus BMW's StartupGarage was based on the notion of the venture client, whereby selected startups would have BMW as one of their first clients. Others say that it's better for a large corporation to partner with startups (without an equity investment) or to acquire them outright, should they be strategically relevant. My view is that CVC has a useful role to play in terms of strategic investments in fairly mature startups – and that non-equity partnering will continue to be important for relatively earlier-stage startups. In either case, as Brady pointed out, what's important is the

> *need for a partnering orientation. And that's likely to distinguish the wheat from the chaff when it comes to CVC investors.*
>
> **Shameen Prashantham**, *professor of international business and strategy, China Europe International Business School*

Cottage business

Also known as a lifestyle business, this refers to any business that's created or being run to give the owners and employees sufficient revenue to maintain the lifestyle and scale of business they want, without having to think about raising investment capital to grow and scale in a less profitable way.

Covenant

A clause in an agreement or contract that states that an individual or company will or will not do certain things. A non-compete clause that restricts an employee from working for a competitor for a fixed period of time is an example of a restrictive covenant that's frequently included in employment agreements.

Coworking space

A space where workers from different companies share an office, allowing cost savings and convenience through the use of common facilities such as equipment, utilities and receptionist services. Examples of coworking providers are WeWork and TOG (The Office Group).

Crowdfunding

The practice of funding a programme, project or venture by raising small amounts of money from a large number of people, typically via specialist online platforms such as Kickstarter, Crowdcube and Seedrs.

Cryptography

This is associated with the process of securely converting ordinary plain text into unintelligible text and vice versa. It involves the storing and transmission of data in a particular form so that only those for whom it's intended are able to read and process it. Cryptography is used to protect data from alteration and theft and to confirm user authentication when required.

Cryptocurrency

A digital or virtual currency secured by cryptography, which makes it almost impossible to hack, counterfeit or double-spend. Bitcoin is considered to be the first cryptocurrency.

Customer acquisition cost (CAC)

This measures how much an organisation needs to spend in terms of resources and costs to acquire a new customer. It's a key metric for investors. The relationship between CAC and LTV is critical, as the ratio between the two can have a major impact on a company's ability to achieve scale and profitability. Likewise, CAC can have a major impact on a company's runway and burn rate.

Daily active users (DAU)

The number of unique users that interact with a product (eg an app) within a one-day window.

Deal flow

A term used by investors and others to describe a flow of investment opportunities. This is usually a combination of inbound/cold emails, deals that emerge from investors' existing networks of friends, portfolio companies and others, as well as any proprietary deal flow they may have through private networks, university relationships and more.

Decentralised autonomous organisation (DAO)

A community-led entity that runs online via blockchain, governed entirely by its individual members rather than the traditional central authority of a board of members or executives.

Decentralised applications (DAPP)

Also known as dApps or dapps, these are digital applications that run on a blockchain. Due to their decentralised nature, DAPPs provide many privacy advantages, as users don't need to submit personal information to use the product, relying instead on smart contracts.

Deal lead

An individual at a VC fund who is the designated champion of the deal. On most occasions this will be the principal or partner, who leads on the communications with the company and acts as their internal advocate within the fund. The deal lead also defines the deal terms such as investment amount, valuation and more.

Deal structure

The terms of an agreement between a company and their investors. For most startups, deals are either priced (or equity) rounds or convertible note rounds, with a smaller number involving a combination of both. The deal structure also includes the rights and responsibilities that the startup and investor undertake.

Debt financing

A type of financing where a company borrows money to manage the business rather than financing through equity (the issuing of shares). Examples of debt financing are bank loans, personal loans and credit cards. In the case of startups, debt financing usually comes from specific venture debt funds and companies as well as from companies such as Clearbanc and Uncapped, which deal in revenue and inventory-based funding.

Decacorn

A company worth in excess of $10 billion. Decacorn is a portmanteau of unicorn (a company with a billion-dollar-plus valuation) and deca (meaning ten, from the Greek *deka*).

Decentralised finance (DeFi)

A blockchain-based form of finance that doesn't rely on central financial intermediaries such as banks and exchanges to offer traditional financial instruments. DeFi leverages smart contracts on blockchains, the most common for this purpose being Ethereum.

Decentralised web

Also known as DWeb, this is similar to the World Wide Web that we know, but doesn't rely on centralised operators (Facebook or Google, for example). Individuals will own the content that they post and can control and benefit from it financially.

Deepfake

A synthetic piece of media (audio, images, video or text) that uses machine learning and AI to replicate or replace a person's likeness, voice or writing. The term is typically associated with negative uses of this technology, such as creating audio to replicate someone's voice or a video of someone's likeness to spread misinformation. However, there are more positive uses of the technology as well, as it's regularly used in the film and TV industries to replicate an actor's voice from the past, or to digitally de-age an actor.

Deep tech (aka hard tech)

A term used to describe highly sophisticated and advanced technology, usually rooted in scientific principles and engineering innovations. Deep tech builds on years of extensive research and development, making it completely different from more mainstream technology (sometimes known as shallow tech). Examples of deep tech areas are AI, advanced materials, blockchain, aerospace, biotechnology and life sciences, robotics, drones, photonics and quantum computing.

Demo day

This usually happens at the end of accelerator programmes, although there are several online versions that are run separately. Demo day is an online or virtual event where a number of companies that are part of an accelerator cohort or other group have an opportunity to pitch or demo their products and services to an external audience. The primary audience of these demo days are angel investors and VCs, although in many cases a wider group of attendees are involved.

Dilution

When a company raises capital or allocates some shares to an option pool or co-founder, the resulting decrease in the shareholding of other shareholders is referred to as dilution. For example, in a business that raises a $1 million pre-seed round at a $5 million post-money valuation (ie after investment has been made), the existing shareholders will be diluted by 20 per cent.

Dilution protection

A clause in a term sheet or investment agreement that protects an investor's stake in the company from dilution in a subsequent round or rounds of investment. (See also: Anti-dilution provision.)

Direct to consumer (DTC)

A subset of the B2C market. The term is generally used to refer to companies that sell physical products to customers on a one-off or subscription basis. For the most part, these brands are digital first in that they don't have a physical retail location where customers can try or test the product before they buy. Some well-known examples of DTC brands include the footwear brand Allbirds, the subscription food companies HelloFresh and Kencko, and the mattress company Casper.

DTC businesses are wonderful when they work well but can be notoriously difficult to get off the ground, especially in a crowded marketplace with fickle consumers.

When you have a scaling DTC business, you receive valuable data about consumer habits, behaviours, trends and need states. You can see in real time the outcome of your decisions, what works and what doesn't, and it can be a really fertile environment in which to get feedback and test and learn as you go.

However, to be successful, you have to know your customer well – why do they want your product/ service, why is it better than any other, how much are they willing to spend, how many times a week/ month/year? In-depth research on your customer base is essential and a constant, ongoing cycle of feedback and implementation is critical.

Having a strong DTC business can also enable a pivot into B2B models, as other businesses want to access your customer base and brand value. So, building a strong DTC business to start with can enable longer term sustainability and business model diversification further down the line.

This was something we did with BritBox International (a subscription streaming service for British TV shows abroad). We started with DTC customers as our beachhead market, but to access a wider customer pool that wouldn't come to us directly, we formed a partnership with Amazon Channels in the US, and carriage deals with other digital TV services in the Nordics and Australia to diversify our revenue streams and expand our market footprint.

Serena Martin, *ex BBC, Sky and BritBox International; startup mentor and advisor*

Disclosure document

A legal document exchanged by founders and investors that discloses any potential issues that could have an impact on the company or investment. For example, if a company is in debt or being sued, they would need to inform an investor in a disclosure document or letter. This is closely related to an NDA.

Discounted cash flow (DCF)

A method used to value a business that estimates the present value of a company based on projected future cash flows. DCF analysis involves forecasting future cash flows and discounting them to their present value using a discount rate that reflects the risk of the investment.

Disruptors

Many tech companies are (or think of themselves as) disruptors, in that they come into an existing market or segment of the economy and apply technology to speed up processes or make them more efficient. In doing so, they rapidly gain market share and disrupt the incumbents in that space. One of the best examples of this is how Uber and other ride-hailing apps disrupted the more traditional taxi medallion and licence markets around the world.

Distributed ledger technology (DLT)

A secure digital system for recording the transaction of assets in which the transactions and their respective details are recorded in numerous places at the same time. Unlike traditional databases, distributed ledgers have no central data store or administration functionality. Blockchain is a well-known example of a distributed ledger technology.

Double bottom line (DBL/2BL)

A metric that covers not only the traditional bottom line, such as profitability or growth, but also an additional one that's related to how much of a positive social impact a business is having. One of the best-known examples of this is Ben & Jerry's ice cream, which had both business and social objectives – profit and community impact.

Down round

A round of funding raised by a startup where the valuation is lower than the valuation in the previous round of funding. Many companies (such as Soundcloud, Flipkart, Foursquare and TaskRabbit) have had down rounds. In general, the founders and team, as well as previous investors, suffer substantial dilution in a down round scenario, particularly if there are anti-dilution clauses in any of the previous investment documents.

In the life of a tech founder, raising a funding round is usually synonymous with success, and tends to indicate growth. So, when one hears the words down round for the first time, introduced by existing or (worse) potential investors, it's as if an earthquake just shook them to their core! They are dirty words, like black clouds heralding the inevitable doom – the end of the growth trajectory of their company. That same growth is so dearly desired but, if we're being honest, most of the time it's forced upon them by the tech industry and its virtuous/vicious circle of ever-increasing valuations. But if you think about it (and it's oh-so-easy from the outside), a down round can often be a lifeline for an otherwise dying company. So, yes, it's hard to hear, but down rounds are often a blessing in disguise, a much-needed reset, and a way to refocus the strategy and restart the business on a new path towards success.

One such company I invested in and supported along the way got pushed by institutional investors into a very high valuation too quickly without the validation of the market. It was a classic case of 'too fast go-to-market' with 'not enough of a product/ market fit'. This resulted in a battle to the bottom on the next down round as no one was ready to invest so high. Fast forward a year, and the company is in much better shape than before, with more potential to grow than they ever thought possible. Not so bad after all.

Raph Crouan, *founder and CEO, DisruptVenture Ltd; president, French Tech London*

Downstream integration

Also known as forward integration, this is a business strategy that's used when a company looks to own or control activities that are down the line in the value chain (ie control of its distribution or logistics activities). Perhaps the most well-known example of this is Amazon. It started as a marketplace that held no stock, simply passing the orders on to publishers. Three years later, the company made the decision to rent a warehouse and own stock. Now, it has its own delivery fleets of aircraft and trucks.

Drag-along rights

See: Tag-along rights.

Drive-by deal

This is where an investor puts capital into a company in the hope of a fast return. These deals typically happen at the pre-IPO stage, when a return is all but guaranteed. They generally involve minimal due diligence and partici- pation/support by the VC or investor in question.

Dry powder

A term used to refer to the unallocated capital that's being managed by venture capital funds. For example, if a £50 million fund has invested £10 million in startups, it can be said to have £40 million in dry powder.

Due diligence

A process that investors and others follow to dig into the structure of a company. It's generally run by VC and angel investors to look at the accounts, legal agreements and other data that a business holds before deciding to make an investment. As a rule, this happens at the final stages of the investment decision process. Think of it as a background check on you, your company and your business to date. Due diligence (or DD, as many refer to it) is usually light in early-stage investments, but becomes increasingly detailed as the size of investment increases.

> *In the context of investing, due diligence is the process the prospective interested parties will follow to collect, analyse and verify information prior to confirming a decision to proceed with an agreement. It's common to see the statement 'subject to due diligence' on a term sheet or letter of intent, and there should also be a time frame in which this is expected to be completed. Depending on the stage, size, industry and complexity of the investment, due diligence can be a relatively quick process, but can sometimes be a long and expensive exercise.*
>
> *Investors and investment committees will want to read a due diligence opinion prior to approving their*

decision to move forward, and this opinion will be based on information collected from the seller as well as independently, including verification of revenues, accounts receivable and payable, intellectual property, information technology, customer feedback, competitive analysis, legal status, claims made by the seller, inventory levels, outstanding and potential liabilities, employee status, founder stability, KYC (know your customer) of previous investors and perceived reliability of forecasts related to the future as well as audit confirmation of data provided. Depending on the sector, there may be specific subject matter expert verifications, for example of the viability of a technology or the probability a patent will stand up when contested in court.

Today, many of the requests for due diligence can be managed online in what are referred to as virtual data rooms (VDRs). The seller can securely upload data into a VDR and then verify who accessed this data and when. Data provided in the VDR may be attached to the share purchase agreement and be referenced in representations and warranties provided by the seller. Companies, particularly those with funding in venture capital, frequently pre-prepare a VDR for access by potential investors.

Scott Newton, *managing partner, Thinking Dimensions*

Early adopters

These are the first users of a product. They're often key influencers who are active on social media and tend to offer you brutally honest and direct feedback. If you can identify these people effectively and interact with them at an early stage, you can expect plenty of free brand exposure through personal endorsements and recommendations.

Early exit

This is when startup owners sell their ownership before they planned to, rather than when the business is at growth stage. This could often be to liquidate financial assets to safely exit from the market and minimise losses, or to take advantage of earlier-than-expected gains. In other instances, an early exit takes place when a company is building a product or technology that a larger or equivalent company wants to buy as quickly as possible.

Early stage

Companies in this category are usually within their first 12-18 months and are still trying to achieve product/market fit. In many cases, they're trying to raise funding, build an MVP, secure patents, attract initial customers or partnerships, or move from an idea through alpha and beta release versions of their product.

Earn-out clause

This is a common feature of merger and acquisition (M&A) deals. An earn-out clause applies when a percentage of the agreed sale price is deferred until a later date, and is released based on specific durations of time or other KPIs being met. These could be financial or growth metrics. Earn-out clauses are generally included to create an incentive for the founders and team members of the company being acquired to remain at the acquiring company for a sufficient period of time to ensure a full and successful handover and transition.

EBITDA

An acronym used mostly in accounting and financial contexts. It stands for earnings before interest, tax, depreciation and amortisation. It's typically used as a measure of your core corporate profitability and is calculated by subtracting all the costs of the operating business (wages, materials, services, etc) from the company's revenues. It doesn't include a decline in asset value, loan/lease expenses or any tax/government payment obligations.

Edge computing

A computing model that brings storage and computing power closer to the user. This allows applications or products to run faster, rather than relying on fully cloud-based computing. Currently, it's most frequently used in descriptions of IoT (internet of things) devices, where data is processed 'on the edge', meaning on the device. One well-known application of edge computing is Apple's Face ID, where the device's camera captures a 3D map of a user's face. That data is then processed on the device and compared to scans in order to unlock the device.

Effective accelerationism (e/acc)

E/acc is a largely philosophical movement that argues for embracing rapid technological progress (in particular with regard to AI) to solve some of the world's major problems. The core ideas include the inevitability of technological change, as well as the argument that we should embrace this rather than resisting it. It's an emerging school of thought, so this definition is one that will evolve over the coming months and years.

Elevator pitch

A brief presentation that features a clear idea for a product, service or project. The name originates from the pitch being delivered in the time it takes to ride in an elevator, which is usually about 30 seconds. The objective is to make sure you're ready to share key facts with anyone at any time in an attempt to convince others you have an idea worth investing in.

> *The elevator pitch is the initial flirtation in the courtship between company and investor. It's the first - but potentially most crucial - step in the fundraising journey.*
>
> *An effective elevator pitch persuades the investor to take an email. The cover email inspires the investor to open the pitch deck. The pitch deck warrants a*

> *meeting. The meeting motivates the arrangement of a second meeting, joined by colleagues. The second meeting leads to a review of the data room materials. The data room materials warrant reference checks and follow-up meetings. References and meetings lead to more intensive due diligence. Due diligence results in a term sheet. The term sheet guides the legal negotiation. The legal negotiation culminates with money in the bank and a new marriage of company and investor. But it all starts with the elevator pitch.*
>
> **Daniel Glazer**, *London managing partner, Wilson Sonsini*

Enshittification

This term was coined by the author and activist Cory Doctorow. Voted the 2023 word of the year by the American Dialect Society, it was described by its creator in a recent *Financial Times* piece as 'a three-stage process: first, platforms are good to their users. Then they abuse their users to make things better for their business customers. Finally, they abuse those business customers to claw back all the value for themselves. Then, there is a fourth stage: they die.'

> *In his essay (see on.ft.com/3JHtqz8), Doctorow is talking about the big tech companies. The user experience on platforms and apps is getting worse and worse: the ads, suggested follows and grey goo of AI-generated nonsense that fill every feed; the large retailers who launch own-brand versions of*

products they see doing well on their platform; or the stochastic parrots [see separate entry] of the LLM and chatbot world that produce convincing-looking language without ever truly understanding what they're talking about.

One of my overarching goals in life is to avoid becoming the old man yelling at a cloud, but it's hard to get around a real fear that the 'enshittocene' era that we've entered isn't just limited to those big online platforms, but is extending its tentacles into all aspects of our lives. From wars, blockades and elections to the circulation collapse in the Atlantic Ocean, there are days when the headlines are enough to make you want to pull a Homer (Simpson), hide under a pile of coats and hope that somehow everything will work out.

That's just the news. That's before we get to deepfake phishing, which has me creating safe phrases to use with my family in case an algorithmically generated version of me calls up looking for bail money. In a year (2024) where half the world will vote in elections that could have seismic impacts on climate, conflict and our safety and sanity, it's hard to escape the creeping feeling that we're all Neo (from The Matrix) on the train tracks, listening to the sound of inevitability.

Eamonn Carey, *general partner, Tera Ventures*

Enterprise

An alternative name for a business or corporation.

Enterprise Investment Scheme (EIS)

A UK government scheme designed to encourage investment in early-stage private companies. Typically used by angels and VCTs, EIS investments entitle the investor to several tax incentives, including the ability to write off 30 per cent of the value of the investment against their tax bill, further tax relief on any losses incurred, exemption from capital gains tax on profits realised, and more. Companies that raise funds using EIS have often previously raised using SEIS.

Entrepreneur-in-residence

A (usually short-term) position taken on by successful serial entrepreneurs in between startups or ventures, often at a venture capital fund, to understand the VC side, build their network and gain access to new opportunities. The role often includes seeking out and vetting startups, acting as a consultant on portfolio companies and involvement in deals with the investment team.

Equity financing

The procedure by which capital is raised through selling company shares to the public, institutional or financial investors. This differs from convertible note rounds, as the price per share and valuation of the company is clearly defined in advance and makes it clear what dilution founders, team members, existing investors and others will take.

Equity kicker

In some cases where companies are raising venture debt or other forms of later-stage financing, funds can add in a requirement for equity in the company alongside the return of the principal loan amount and any interest incurred. In most cases, this results in a slightly reduced interest rate or other preferential terms.

Escrow

A legal concept whereby an asset or escrow money is held by a third party on behalf of two other parties that are in the process of completing a transaction. These escrow assets/fees will then be released when receiving the appropriate instructions from the respective parties and/or until the fulfilment of predetermined contractual obligations.

Ether (ETH)

The cryptocurrency of the Ethereum network is one of the most popular and frequently used cryptocurrencies alongside Bitcoin. Ether was originally started as a cryptocurrency that would be complementary to Bitcoin, but has grown substantially in its own right.

Ethereum blockchain

A blockchain platform with its own cryptocurrency called Ether (ETH) or Ethereum, and its own programming language called Solidity.

Ethical AI

A term used to describe the development and use of AI that has fairness, transparency, accountability and human wellbeing at its core. According to UNESCO, AI systems should be auditable and traceable. There should be oversight, impact assessment, audit and due diligence mechanisms in place to avoid conflicts with human rights norms and threats to environmental wellbeing.

Evergreen

A fund that's regularly replenished – either via cash flow or limited partners – rather than one that has to raise capital every three to five years. Many corporate VC funds are evergreen, with their investment capital coming off the balance sheet. Likewise, family offices and ultra high net worth individual funds don't have external limited partners or investors so could be classed as evergreen.

Exit

This occurs when a startup or business sells some or all of its company to another business. In most cases, this means the whole company is acquired, including assets and team members. The goal for most investors is an exit that provides the highest possible return on their investment.

Exit strategy

A plan that lays down how a business owner plans to sell their company to give them and their investors the best possible return on their investment. This can be in the form of an IPO, a trade sale, M&A, a fire sale and more.

Explainable AI (XAI)

Sometimes shortened to XAI, explainable AI is an AI with logic that can be interpreted by humans, allowing people to understand the process used to reach specific decisions. In many cases, this involves training an AI to 'speak' in plain language and with clear reasoning. An example of explainable AI in a financial setting is a lending algorithm that could explain to an applicant why they have or haven't been approved for a loan based on the data available to and analysed by the AI.

F

Fire sale

A term used to describe the urgent sale of a company or its assets at a price that's far below its market value. This most often happens when a company is running out of capital and wants to avoid liquidation or receivership.

First-mover advantage

Simply defined as a company's ability to be better off than its competitors as a result of being the first to market in a new product category/sector.

> *'First to market wins.' This is the advice of Leonard Lauder in his 2020 book* The Company I Keep: My life in beauty. *I've seen this myself, and more than nine years after founding SoPost, I'm experiencing the benefits of being first on a daily basis. Because our company was so unique in what we offered, I had a major advantage: the only thing I needed to do was convince brands that they should be distributing product samples online rather than through more conventional channels. If they agreed with my reasoning, it was pretty much a given that SoPost would be the partner they'd do it with. After all, there weren't really any viable alternatives. This meant that we won more business than if we were in a crowded market, or if we were the second, third or*

fourth company to enter the space. And, of course, everything compounds. Because our success rate was so high, we grew a lot faster than we otherwise would have.

Our advantage endures to this day. We have a reputation as the leading company in our space, and our head start means that we have more data with which to build incredible experiences, more insight into the market and, frankly, the greatest drive to keep innovating. While we're building the future of product sampling, all I see from those following in our footsteps are hasty attempts to catch up. I know who I'd bet on to win.

Jonathan Grubin, *founder and CEO, SoPost*

Flat round

A round of raising finance that's closed at the same valuation as the startup's previous round of financing. In many cases, this happens as part of a bridge round, or in cases where a company has been unable to deliver on some KPIs that they promised in their conversations with previous round investors.

Founder burnout

A form of exhaustion caused by constantly feeling overwhelmed when founding and building a business from scratch. Like other forms of burnout, it happens as a direct result of excessive and prolonged emotional, mental and physical stress.

This founder burnout story started at 2 am one day, when an ambulance had to be called because, despite being 36 and healthy, I was experiencing chest pain. At the time, my co-founder and I were running our second startup (we'd had a small exit from the first) and our marketing tech was being used by brands such as Vodafone, Expedia and Samsung. Unbeknown to me at the time, this was the first sign that I had a form of post-traumatic stress caused by the relentless pace and pressure to perform that I put myself under as a founder. By the point of diagnosis 17 months later, I was having completely unprompted panic attacks, even while walking my dog in the park.

This is just one story, but it turns out mine was far from the only one. According to the Entrepreneur Pressure & Wellbeing Report 2019, nine out of ten founders show signs of mental health strain, with 78 per cent believing that running their business has affected their mental health and 68 per cent experiencing regular sleep issues. If this isn't enough, almost everyone believes they're the only one struggling with challenges as a founder, leaving eight out of ten alone on the entrepreneurial roller coaster. As founders, we all know we need to set ourselves up for a marathon, not a sprint, but these stats stop us from going the distance. That's why we created FounderCircles, intimate and safe coaching spaces for founders to problem-solve together, share knowledge and support each other, stopping loneliness in its tracks and creating real connection that fuels founders to be resilient and thrive, not just survive on the journey.

Christina Richardson, *founder, weare3Sixty*

Founder/market fit

A phrase used by some investors to talk about the experience a founder has in the sector in which they're doing business. For example, someone who has been a lawyer for ten years and is now starting a legal tech business to address a problem they faced in their career would be deemed to have strong founder/market fit.

Fractional

A fractional role is another term for a part-time or temporary worker. It's generally used to refer to someone slightly more senior in a business. Perhaps the most frequent example is a fractional CFO.

> *Fractional consulting offers a unique solution for businesses in the changing fields of technology, digital innovation and the creative industries. As someone who has worked as a growth and innovation consultant, I've had the opportunity to collaborate with a wide range of companies and have seen first hand how fractional consultants play a pivotal role in driving sustainable growth and fostering innovation.*
>
> *In the fast-paced world of technology and the digital sectors, having access to high-level, specialist strategic guidance is essential. However, not all businesses have the means (or budget) to hire full-time executives. This is where fractional consulting comes in as a real game changer. It allows companies to tap into the expertise of industry veterans on a part-time or project basis, giving them access to*

insights and leadership without bearing the burden of full-time executive salaries.

In my opinion, the beauty of consulting lies in its flexibility and scalability. Businesses can tailor their level of engagement based on their needs and growth stages. Whether it's navigating through transformation, developing marketing strategies, optimising financial operations or guiding product development, fractional consultants bring a wealth of experience, fresh perspectives and best practices from working across various sectors. They inject ideas and approaches into businesses that can help to accelerate growth and enhance their advantage.

In summary, for companies operating in the technology, digital and creative industries, where agility and innovation play a role, fractional consultancy provides a unique opportunity to leverage high-calibre executive expertise. It empowers businesses to maintain flexibility, swiftly adapt to market dynamics and concentrate on their core strengths while effectively managing costs.

Fractional consultancy goes beyond being a service; it creates a partnership that nurtures growth, fosters innovation, ensures long-term success and is an opportunity that I'd strongly recommend business founders to consider.

Naomi Timperley, *co-founder, Tech North Advocates*

Fund of funds

An investment vehicle that invests in other VC or private equity investment vehicles. The goal of these funds is to achieve a broad degree of diversification of the types of funds or investments they're making across multiple sectors and asset classes.

Funding round

Used to describe the rounds of funding that startups go through to raise capital, with each round involving the business accepting at least one investment from at least one investor within a specific time period.

Fungible token

In cryptocurrency terms, a fungible token refers to a uniform token that can be exchanged with other, similar cryptocurrencies. The cryptocurrency Bitcoin is a common example of a digital fungible token, where if you send somebody a bitcoin and they send you one back, it doesn't need to be the same bitcoin. This same concept of fungibility exists with fiat currencies as well. If you give someone a £5 note, they can repay you with any other £5 note rather than having to give you back the original one you gave them.

Futurecorn

A fast-growing business set to achieve unicorn status and gain a $1 billion valuation. Most futurecorns are valued between $250 million and $1 billion. They are sometimes known as soonicorns.

Game-Fi

An amalgam of gaming and decentralised finance, which is sometimes referred to as 'play to earn'. The vast majority of these games are blockchain based and supported by an in-game currency, a marketplace and a unique token economy, which is usually managed and governed by the community itself.

Gas

Every transaction on Ethereum requires gas, which is a small amount of ETH paid to the network. Gas is the fuel that powers Ethereum and is measured in gwei, a small denomination of ETH. So-called gas costs on the Ethereum blockchain have given rise to a variety of competitive cryptocurrencies and blockchains, many with more environmentally and financially sustainable goals.

Generative adversarial network (GAN)

A type of machine learning model that involves two neural networks 'competing' against one another. The generator network creates new data using an existing training dataset, which can include images, text, etc. The discriminator network then tries to function as an adversary or critic, trying to distinguish between the real and generated data. By doing so, the generator network needs to create increasingly realistic data, and the discriminator becomes more adept at detecting fakes. This process means both networks continually improve over time. One of the best-known consumer applications of GANs is the reduction of blur or distortion in old photos. In this case, The generator network takes a blurry image and tries to make it sharp enough to fool the discriminator network. The discriminator network learns to tell the difference between a real sharp image and the generator's attempts to clean up blurry ones.

Generative AI

A form of AI that can create new and original items or data based on training datasets. Examples of generative AI include image generators such as Dall-E and Midjourney, which allow users to enter a text prompt that then creates a corresponding image or images. Similarly, ChatGPT is a form of generative AI, as its conversations are new and original but have their origins in the dataset created by OpenAI over time. GAI (or GenAI) is not to be confused with AGI – see Artificial general intelligence.

Generative pre-trained transformer (GPT)

A form of AI that has the ability to understand, analyse and create content that's similar to text written by humans. The technology uses machine learning to process large volumes of data and learn relevant patterns from it. The most famous example of a GPT is OpenAI's ChatGPT, which uses this technology for its chatbot service.

General partner (GP)

A manager at a venture capital fund who raises capital for the fund, sources and does deals and makes decisions about how to allocate the capital being managed by the fund. In most cases, a general partner will also have so-called 'skin in the game', meaning they will invest their own money into the fund alongside their LPs. Most funds have two or more general partners but a recent trend has been towards 'solo GPs' who manage funds on their own.

GPT-3/4/5

GPT-3/4/5 and any future iterations/numbers are generative pre-trained transformer models released by Open AI. They're most frequently used in the context of being the model used by ChatGPT.

Ground floor

The term used to describe the very beginning of a venture or startup. Many investors will talk about getting into a company on the ground floor to denote how early they became involved in a company or sector.

Grounding (in AI)

This is when a model is given access to physical objects, a shared knowledge base or other information to give it additional context, which in turn will make its responses more relevant. Grounding therefore ensures that a specific model's understanding is more closely linked to the real world. For example, an AI recipe generation model can generate infinite recipes. A grounded model with access to your fridge, pantry, equipment and more could be far more specific about the recipes it recommends.

Growth hacking

A term first coined by Sean Ellis of Dropbox to describe a marketing technique that focuses on quickly finding scalable growth through non-traditional and inexpensive tactics such as making use of mailing lists, referral programmes or social media. Airbnb, Uber, Zynga and others made great use of several of these techniques.

> *Growth hacking could easily be the most overused phrase in this lexicon. Beware the snake oil surrounding the term and its seductive promises of hypergrowth. But what is a good growth hacker and what do they do? This is a type of marketer in a startup whose primary focus is growth. Their skill sets are different to a traditional marketer as they'll a) integrate with tech and product to iterate offerings quickly to find routes to growth; and b) they'll explore every possible technical lever the business has to find that: SEO, pricing strategies, partnerships, referrals, virality and, frankly, anything that'll do the job.*
>
> *One of the first growth hacks was Hotmail's 'PS: I Love You' offer of a free Hotmail signup for a user's friends. I firmly believe that every startup has its own unique hack, somewhere. It may not be as stratospheric as Hotmail's but it's worth the investment of time to explore beyond the obvious.*
>
> *I've seen it at work at MPowder, a menopause supplement business I invest in. They realised the strength of feeling among their early customer base*

and created a sandbox space on Facebook for text messaging, products, pricing and recipes. This hyper-engaged community became a referrals powerhouse as the business grew and later led to MPowder's distribution in the major supermarkets.

Take the time to investigate. Focus on the methodological testing, not just the fireworks. Know that, at some point, you're going to need a more 'brand' oriented marketer, too.

Barney Worfolk-Smith, *MD EMEA DAIVID, venture partner at Ascension Ventures; independent investor*

H

Hallucination (in AI)

A hallucination happens when generative AI analyses content but generates incorrect information and presents it as fact. While hallucinations can sometimes be interesting, they're undesirable outcomes and usually indicate a problem in the generative model's outputs.

When we hear the word hallucination, we usually think of seeing or hearing things that aren't really there, right? In the world of AI, it's a bit different but kind of similar. Imagine AI as a super creative storyteller. It's been fed loads of information and stories from all over the internet. Now, when you ask it something, it uses all that knowledge to create a robust response.

The hallucination part comes in when AI gets a bit too creative or makes mistakes. Sometimes it creates information that seems real but just isn't. It's not lying on purpose; it's just that its way of trying to understand the world can lead to some pretty wild answers.

Let's say you ask AI about a historical event such as the moon landing. Most of the time, it'll give you accurate info. But occasionally, it might mix up dates or even invent a fictional astronaut. It's not trying to deceive; it's just connecting dots in a way that makes sense to its algorithm but not necessarily to reality.

Or, if you ask about a scientific concept, AI might give you an explanation that sounds super plausible but is actually a blend of different facts that it 'knows', creating a new 'fact' that doesn't really exist.

In a nutshell, hallucinations are like creative slip-ups where AI mixes and matches its vast bank of information in ways that can be unexpectedly false or imaginative. However, in my experience, hallucinations have become one of the most intriguing aspects of marketing content creation. You lay out a plan, aiming for a certain narrative, and then AI throws in something totally unexpected. Initially, it felt like navigating a maze blindfolded but I've since learned to appreciate these moments. The key? Embracing the process of iteration. It's amazing how an AI-generated curveball can, with a little patience, become a goldmine for creativity. And, to be honest, some of AI's wilder ideas have also given me quite a few laughs along the way!

Jill Rudnick, *marketing advisor, Rudnick Ventures*

Hardware as a service (HAAS)

Here, rather than purchasing it, the customer pays for the services provided by the hardware. In essence, the customer pays for the value provided by the hardware versus owning the hardware itself. Examples include cab and bike rental services.

Hockey stick

An expression used by investors to describe the shape of the growth curve they want to see in the businesses in which they invest. They want their startups to be growing quickly and at least doubling sales year on year. In some cases, this can be referred to as a J curve.

Human in the loop (HITL)

A phrase used in the context of machine learning. It's most often used to describe the process of combining machine and human intelligence to obtain a desired result. This combination can be used during the training and testing phases of an AI model but can also prove invaluable during the 'live and in-market' phase as well. An example of HITL is content moderation systems, where posts and images can be removed automatically by an AI agent but can also be viewed and approved or denied by a human.

Immutable

An immutable ledger in blockchain refers to records that remain unchanged, ie they can't be altered or amended. In essence, blockchain itself is an immutable database, where you can't change or manipulate the data that's already in the blockchain.

Incubator

An organisation set up to support early-stage startups with the intention of helping them grow their businesses, progress and succeed. For the most part, incubators work with companies at the ideation stage before a product or team has been fully created.

Initial public offering (IPO)

A sale of company stock to the public for the first time on a recognised stock exchange. Before an IPO, the company will be considered private; afterwards, it becomes a publicly listed company.

The phrase 'company goes public on Nasdaq/NYSE/ LSE' is more commonly used and maybe more commonly understood. An IPO was initially built to help companies raise a significant amount of capital to scale a business. With the rise of larger pools of private capital, where VC funds and PE funds can *easily fund $1 billion+ rounds, IPOs became more of an exit tool to shareholders and early investors rather than the source of large growth capital. Nevertheless, IPOs are an essential part of the capital circle and provide the opportunity to exit with large gains to shareholders and, with this, introduce new investors to the market. An IPO is also a great way to raise capital from public investors while giving access to high-growth (tech) companies to a larger investor base. During the IPO process, a company's structure will be changed from a private limited company to a public limited company. This, along with information disclosure and expectations on publicly listed companies, sets new standards for companies that have been thus far privately run and funded. It requires strong maturity from companies to go for the IPO.*

Kaidi Ruusalepp, *founder and CEO, Funderbeam*

Institutional investors

Entities such as VC funds, hedge funds, mutual funds and others. Typically, they invest capital that's pooled from multiple limited partners or other sources. Historically, institutional investors have been investors in later-stage rounds of a company's growth, but they're increasingly investing in the pre-seed and seed stage.

Investor FAQ

A lightweight and easy-to-manage tool to support your prospective investors, existing investors and colleagues to stay informed and help you close your round and get back to growing your business. Investor FAQs can be included in pitch presentations or hosted online to provide easy access to the frequently asked questions that companies will get as they go through the fundraising process.

> *At SAP.iO Foundry, powered by Techstars Accelerator, we organised a series of great investor workshops with a number of leading Berlin VCs and our companies. The format was a private 'ask me anything' (AMA) style fireside chat/workshop where our founders could ask the 'stupid' questions and get personal tips and advice on how to raise money from industry veterans.*
>
> *We covered several of the expected topics, such as how to get introductions, the importance of researching your investors and how important it is to prepare your materials in advance (more on this later). But when one investor (the awesome Ricardo Sequerra from Cherry Ventures) talked about the power of a 'Dynamic Investor FAQ' document, I was sold. Ricardo told a story about a London-based founder whom he felt was a master at fundraising. The founder had very effectively used a live Google Doc as their investor FAQ to help win over more investors and build more momentum in their round.*
>
> *Here's how it worked.*
> *Every time the founder met with an investor, they kept track of the new and unexpected questions they'd received.*
> *As this was usually a new question, the founder would often forget to include some important detail*

in their initial answer or else they'd think of a much better answer after the meeting when chatting with their other co-founders and mentors.

Rather than leaving the investor to just rely on their original answer, the founder would then spend more time on the answer post-meeting and write up a better, more concise and articulate version of the answer, including any relevant data and links to support it.

They'd then include this answer in their follow-up email to the investor, saying something like, 'Thank you for your time today… really enjoyed it… You asked a great question about X during our meeting and I don't think I did a great job of answering it. Please see the answer I'd have liked to have given you. If you or your colleagues have any other questions, please let me know or you can see our Investor FAQ document here.'

I liked this for four reasons:

1. It helps to build a better impression
The founder used this to recover from an unexpected question and have an excuse to follow up and impress the investor with a better answer later. This shows investors that the founder listened to the question and was quick to follow up (a key skill in fundraising and sales). I like seeing this level of thoughtfulness.

2. It helps to build momentum
Every time a new question arose, it was added to the FAQ document that had been shared with all the other

investors they met. So when the founder was sending out their next email update to prospective investors, they could include a section that was called 'New Investor Questions' added to our FAQ document, with a list of the two or three new questions and a link to the answers in the FAQ. This is a very worthwhile reason to be sending an update… and subtly sends the signal that your round is probably building momentum as you're meeting other investors.

3. It helps your investors sell you internally

Once you move past angel investors, you typically have to convince or interact with an investment firm, which usually consists of other investors and partners that need to be 'sold' by your internal champion. This document helps them sell you when you aren't in the room.

Obviously, no one knows (or should know) the business as well as the founders, so your FAQs help to ensure internal debates are better informed. I've seen firms pull out of deals when they got confused internally on certain core details of a deal and made incorrect assumptions. Yes, this is probably a sign that your internal champion wasn't sufficiently prepared, but people are busy, and a handy FAQ document they can open during a debate can help sway a deal.

Finally, it helps your existing (aka inside) investors when they're pitching you to other investors. I know I sometimes get the details wrong when talking about my portfolio companies, so a handy FAQ would help me when I get questions from investors that I know when I'm trying to pitch your business.

4. It helps you to communicate internally with your team

When I was fundraising, I did a great job of engaging with investors and managing my pipeline. I was focused on the goal and spent weeks away from the office on roadshows to either London, New York or San Francisco. However, I failed miserably at keeping my team updated on progress and all the new questions and answers I was getting from investors. An investor FAQ document like this would've been a great internal communication tool for my team and new hires. It would've helped them get a real picture of what investors were interested in and how the CEO was answering them. Equally, the team could've helped me answer these questions, which would a) have provided better answers to my FAQ; and b) helped the team understand and participate more in the funding process.

Connor Murphy, *founder, Bridge*

Iteration

This describes the continual process of refining an idea or concept. Within the startup world, iteration is crucial, with each small tweak/enhancement leading (hopefully) towards the most optimal solution. Continual feedback loops are an invaluable part of the iteration process, as obtaining live feedback from customers, peers and other related stakeholders is crucial to developing the best final product.

Know your customer (KYC)

A process used by financial institutions and others to verify the identity of their users or customers to prevent fraud, money laundering and more. For example, users may be asked to upload proof of identity (a passport or ID card scan), proof of address (a recent utility bill) or verification of ID (a digital scan of their face) to open a new account at a financial institution.

L

Large action model (LAM)

This term can be understood in two ways. First, as a step beyond a large language model, as it can understand natural language but also take actions based on the user's intent, for example interacting with software and devices on behalf of a user. Second, it can be used in the physical world in a similar context to a large language model. In this definition of a LAM, the AI learns specific physical actions and movements based on the physical actions undertaken by a subject. For example, LAMs can be used in a restaurant setting to allow robots to automate some processes such as cooking burgers, dicing food, etc. Likewise, it can be used in large assembly line or hospital settings to enable robots to perform tasks based on observing videos and visuals of humans performing specific tasks.

Large language models (LLMs)

A large language model is a type of artificial intelligence algorithm that uses deep learning techniques and massive datasets to process, understand, summarise, predict and generate new content. One of the most common use cases is their application in generative AI. For example, the publicly available LLM behind ChatGPT can generate essays, poems and other textual forms in response to user prompts and inputs.

Lead investor

A term used in startup fundraising. The lead investor is typically the individual or fund who negotiates the terms of the investment with the founder/company – setting the investment amount, valuation and other details. While it's usually the case that the lead investor puts in the largest investment in the round, that's not always the case. There can also be a minority lead. It's also usual for the lead investor to be more hands on with the company as a board member or close advisor after the round closes.

Lean startup

A methodology developed by Eric Ries that many founders, entrepreneurs and companies use to build out their ideas and businesses by using continuous improvement and innovation. This often involves heavy engagement with and feedback from their customers or users as they build and iterate on their products. The lean startup methodology emphasises the creation of an MVP, which is a very early, feature-light version of a product that can be shared with alpha and beta testers. The concept is expounded upon at length in the book of the same name.

> The Lean Startup *(Eric Ries, 2011) is an iconic book that outlines how entrepreneurs use continuous innovation to create successful businesses. It has been widely adopted by many in the startup ecosystem and large corporate innovators have recently been treating it as a framework for entrepreneurial endeavours within the enterprise.*

While the lean startup model is rooted in the concept of launching to learn, corporate innovation teams have over-indexed on the pre-MVP experimentation and consumer validation aspect of the framework and failed to launch. The CFO of a Fortune 50 company recently described this as 'experimentation and validation hell'.

A corporate innovation team we worked with were essentially stuck in a loop of validating an endless list of leap-of-faith assumptions. A year of validation had passed before their internal investors asked: 'Where is the MVP?' The team answered by outlining a long list of experiments but failed to show an actual MVP that could be iterated on to find product/market fit. Looking back, the team had gathered enough evidence to support the request for MVP build and launch funding (ie the venture pitch) nearly a year beforehand. The lesson learned here is that the lean startup entrepreneur always has an eye towards going to market. The market always wins, and the sooner you begin incubating in the market, the sooner you'll be able to tell if you're on the path to success.

Andrew Backs, *founder and chief innovation strategist, Pilot44*

Ledger

The public record of transactions on a blockchain. Ledgers are distributed across numerous computers and can be managed by many people, enabling the blockchain to achieve true decentralisation.

Leveraged buyout (LBO)

When a company is acquired (often when a buyer lacks the necessary cash) and a high proportion of the money put into the acquisition is borrowed against the company's assets or cash flow.

Lifetime value (LTV)

Usually used to refer to your customers, the LTV is the average amount of revenue you'll generate from someone over their lifetime as a paying customer of your business.

Limited partner (LP)

An investor in a VC or other fund. Most VC funds raise their capital from LPs, including founders, operators, high net worth individuals, pension funds, corporates, funds of funds and many others. The term can also be used to refer to a part-owner of a company whose individual liability for the company's debts can't exceed the amount they've invested in the company itself.

Liquidation

The process of dissolving or winding down a company by selling off all its assets.

Liquidation preference

A clause or term in investment documents and term sheets that relates to how cash or returns are distributed. In many angel and early-stage rounds, investors receive ordinary shares in the company. Later-stage investors often ask for a 1x liquidation preference, which means that they get their exact initial capital back before any cash is distributed to other investors and shareholders. A 2x liquidation preference would mean any investor with this clause in their investment agreement would get twice their investment back before any capital distributions to other shareholders.

LTV/CAC ratio

An equation used to measure the lifetime value of a customer divided by the customer acquisition cost of acquiring that user. An LTV/CAC of more than three is considered good. Anything less would not be considered positively once you factor in the non-CAC costs of running a business.

> This ratio is a signal of profitability put together from two variables: LTV, which stands for lifetime value; and CAC, which stands for customer acquisition cost. It shows the relationship between the lifetime value of the customer, ie the amount of money you generate from a customer; and the cost of acquiring that customer, ie how much the customer costs the company to become and stay a customer.
>
> SaaS companies in particular aim for a ratio of 3:1 or higher, which indicates that you have a higher ROI (return on investment) for your marketing and sales costs. However, if your ratio is higher, it might mean that you're underspending on your customer acquisition and therefore competitors could gain an advantage to lure your customer away, or you're growing too fast while underspending on marketing.

A lower ratio would indicate that you're spending too much on the acquisition and have a low ROI; it could also indicate a poor product/market fit.

Monitoring this ratio is key to making decisions on investment. As an example, if the ratio is about 5, there's an opportunity to invest more into sales and marketing to support the growth. As a company, you might find it challenging to decide which costs will be attributed towards your CAC, as not all marketing and sales costs are attributed towards acquisition of new customers. Also, when it comes to evaluations, the rule of thumb is that the higher the ratio of LTV to CAC, the higher the valuation, due to higher margins. As a matter of fact, if your LTV to CAC ratio goes from 2x to 3x, it can nearly triple your valuation.

Volker Ballueder, *director, Ballueder Partners Ltd*

Marketplace

A business that facilitates transactions between users. Generally, we think of marketplaces as being two sided – demand and supply. For example, PeskyFish is a UK marketplace where the demand side (consumers and hospitality businesses) can buy directly from the supply side (fishermen and port operators). Some on-demand platforms such as Uber Eats, Postmates and others can be viewed as three sided, with customers, couriers and suppliers all forming part of the value chain.

Mentor

An experienced professional who informally helps to guide a less experienced individual or startup in building their venture.

> *By definition, a mentor is an experienced and trusted advisor. In theory, all three elements – experience, trust, advice – contribute to a well-rounded mentor, but there are additional factors to consider. A well-suited mentor will often be referred through a known and trusted network, have experience from a relevant industry and will value your time, be reliable and communicate effectively. A mentor will challenge you, encourage you and work with you to deliver the best results, often both personally and professionally.*

> *At Level39, we find that mentors are also fantastic navigators across industries and organisations, offering introductions to their network where appropriate.*
>
> *A mentee should be open to learning from a mentor's past mistakes and failures, positively shaping their business journey. When suitably paired, mentee and mentor relationships can be most rewarding. Startups are the creative innovators of tomorrow, but direction and lessons learned are always needed along the way.*

Amy French, *director, Level39*

Metaverse

A term that was first coined by Neal Stephenson in his 1992 sci-fi classic *Snow Crash*. In the book, the metaverse is a virtual world accessed via virtual reality (VR) headsets. The more modern definition maintains that, but also adds in the concept of augmented (AR) and mixed reality. Proponents of the metaverse see a future in which the internet evolves into a 3D world accessible via VR headsets, AR goggles and other devices that allow users to access a fully virtual world or a mixed-reality view of the real world. Games such as *Second Life* were early examples of metaverse concepts, but perhaps the most popular depiction came in Ernest Cline's 2011 science fiction book *Ready Player One* and the 2018 movie directed by Steven Spielberg.

Mezzanine financing

A form of business financing in which the company that's borrowing pays a higher rate of interest than on other loans. However, they have longer to pay back the debt, which may also be converted into shares in the company.

Minimum viable product (MVP)

A new product that's developed with core features only to measure initial response and collect insights to validate the idea and provide input for future product development.

> *In its purest sense, MVP is an idea for a product or service that has been developed into a working solution. Understandably, reaching the MVP stage is an exciting time for the entrepreneur and essential when seeking new investment, as it's the clearest signal that all the hard work has translated into something tangible. Nevertheless, as someone who has devoted many years to getting brands and agencies to adopt new tech, rarely have I seen a product hit MVP and also be a Minimal Viable Business. Inventing something that appears to deliver a problem set by the founder must always be put into the perspective of the end buyer of the product.*
>
> *I'd caution that the investor community threshold for continuing a conversation with an entrepreneur is much lower than for potential clients. Investors can and do get taken in by how 'game-changing' and 'disruptive' the solution is, the back stories of the founders and exponential growth revenue*

projections. People diverting funds from elsewhere to purchase your product are not. They want to know that it solves a real, not perceived, challenge for their business. Therefore, the supply-side evidence of an MVP must be accompanied by strong demand-side proof before founders can honestly say they have a viable business. So, entrepreneurs, when you talk about your MVP to investors and future clients, remember that they're different audiences. For end customers, MVP means evidence of application, proof that your product or service makes a difference (ie real-world case histories), a realistic and relatable pricing model and the confidence that your company has the wherewithal to sustain the inevitable test-and-learn problems. Simply put, the same amount of energy the founders have put into developing a 'working' product must be matched by a thorough understanding of who and why people will want to buy it.

Jim Kite, *founder, Tech Pilot Ltd; former global head, NextTechNow, and of global partnerships, Publicis Media*

Monthly active users (MAU)

A KPI used to count the number of unique users that visit a site or use an app within a month.

N

Non-executive director (NED)

Typically a member of a company's board of directors but not usually an employee of the company. Many companies bring on independent non-executive directors to support them with specific strategic advice as they grow or scale. This can range from general support through to more focused support around key areas such as hiring, tech, international expansion, marketing, sales and more.

Network effects

These occur when the value of a product or service increases as a result of a higher number of users or participants. For example, owning a telephone has no value unless other people also own telephones. Likewise, marketplace platforms such as Etsy and others require network effects to ensure a balance between buyers and sellers.

NFT games

In NFT games, players can swap or trade the in-game NFTs with other players to earn profits. All rules and conditions within NFT games exist within smart contracts.

Non-dilutive funding

A common term used to describe external funding that doesn't require the recipient to give up equity in their company in exchange for the investment. Examples of non-dilutive funding can be government or local enterprise body support grants as well as some philanthropic grants.

> *If starting a business is no simple task, then a technology startup should be… really difficult? The everlasting process of product development, delayed returns on investment and limited development funds present a hurdle, waving a conspicuous red flag to potential investors. This, I believe, is precisely where the significance of non-dilutive funds comes into play, taking the form of friends and family rounds, competitions, tax credits and grants.*
>
> *Non-dilutive funding acts as a crucial avenue to explore during the nascent stages of startup development. It uniquely positions itself by not requiring the startup owner to give up equity prematurely. This translates to the retention of ownership within the founding team for as long as possible, or until it's venture backable or ready for debt funding.*
>
> *Grant funding offers startups the means to cover partial or complete costs associated with product or project development, propelling the idea swiftly up the technology readiness levels while mitigating risks for future investment opportunities. In my experience, this route becomes particularly desirable in sectors such as deep tech, mobility, energy and*

health, where the initial (significant) capital to launch ground-breaking ideas may be limited.

Does grant funding come with any limitations? But of course. It's crucial to dispel any thoughts that grant funding equates to a free or easy infusion of funds into the business. Rather, it comes with specific limitations – for example, the allocation must be directed toward predetermined elements, including labour, subcontractors, material or essential travel. You should also expect stringent due diligence and reporting and almost surgical precision in order to adhere to a minimal variance between projected and actual spend – typically less than 2 per cent in most cases. I repeatedly see the requirement of match funding, which requires the startups to put in anywhere between 10 and 40 per cent of their cash to fund the project. But at the same time, grant funding allows you to extend your runway and test what works in the market and what doesn't. In the world of technology startups, founders rarely have that long runway freedom to test/fail their solutions and that's why non-dilutive funding is often the best way forward.

Agata Bendik, *CEO and co-founder, Pink Brew; senior program manager, Plug and Play*

Non-disclosure agreement (NDA)

A legal contract that sets out an agreement regarding the sharing of information or ideas in confidence. For example, if a startup is considering a partnership with a larger corporate, they may use an NDA so that the startup can share details of their technology, and the corporate can share details of theirs, without fear of either side copying or disclosing any details that may be detrimental to the interests of one or both parties.

Non-fungible token

A token that can be used to demonstrate ownership of unique digital items (eg digital art, music, blogs, tickets). A non-fungible token (NFT) can only have one official owner at a time and is usually secured by the Ethereum blockchain.

Open source

Software that allows its original source code to be made openly available to external developers to redistribute and modify. An example of open source software is WordPress. This is an open source content management system that provides a user-friendly interface to create, organise and publish content on the internet without needing to know how to code. WordPress powers more than 43 per cent of all sites on the internet.

Oversubscription

When companies set out to raise a round of funding, they typically tell investors a specific amount that they're raising. In many cases, they end up receiving more offers of capital than they originally planned for. In these cases, investors think of the round as oversubscribed, and this creates an opportunity for the founder of a company to negotiate the valuation upwards.

Party rounds

A term used to describe funding rounds in which multiple angel investors and VC funds participate. It's frequently used in a negative way, as it implies a lot of people having a good time together rather than something more serious. It's also used to describe highly hyped rounds of funding.

Pay to play

Also known as pay to earn, this requires that an investor continues to contribute to financing to avoid a penalty for discontinuing finance. It's often a conversion of preferred stock into common stock, which provides a strong incentive for investors to participate in future financings.

Peer to peer (P2P)

A decentralised platform on which two individuals can transact directly with each other without the involvement of a third-party intermediary. Some of the most famous examples of P2P businesses include Skype and Napster, as well as more recent examples such as FundingCircle.

Pitch

An opportunity for a startup to present their idea to potential investors, accelerators and entrepreneurs.

The pitch is arguably the most important presentation a startup will have to deliver. A good pitch can lead to many positive outcomes, not least new business and investment opportunities, which are essential ingredients for a successful startup. In contrast, a bad pitch can leave a company treading water, never quite moving forward and eventually running out of opportunities and money. I've witnessed hundreds of startup pitches and facilitated numerous meetings where a startup is only a pitch away from winning lucrative paid work with a large corporate client. In the vast majority of cases, the best pitch wins the deal, but it isn't always the best tech for the job. I've given up predicting which company from those pitching will come out as the winner. There are too many variables in place. However, I can guarantee that if you follow some simple housekeeping rules, you can greatly improve your chances of success.

The rules are simple: rehearse your presentation thoroughly, arrive early, keep to the time requirements, and always, always, leave time for questions. The discussion time after the pitch is just as important as the pitch itself. These rules are simple but often overlooked. In my experience, one of the biggest reasons why a startup that technically should've won the pitch loses is over-presenting (talking too much) and not leaving enough time for questions afterwards.

Losing a pitch because your tech isn't right is one thing; losing it when your tech is perfect but you didn't allow for questions to reconfirm that fact is criminal. Unfortunately, this scenario is not

> uncommon, and many startups are left confused as to why an opportunity that's perfect for their offering has (again) not resulted in any new business.
>
> **Ken Valledy**, *director of startup ecosystems, Antithesis*

Pivot

This is when a company shifts to an alternate business strategy, sometimes completely changing direction and sometimes to address a specific area. This can be due to customer preference, industry changes or an initial strategy that didn't work.

> *The original idea behind SoPost was to create a dynamic postal address linked to your social IDs, so that your address became not where you lived, but where you wanted your post to be sent. The project dates back to 2009, was the main reason I dropped out of university and was pretty much the sole focus of my life for four years. When I launched SoPost, my main objective was to see whether I'd quit uni for the right reason, and if the idea had legs. I quickly ticked the box, as the concept was validated by every stakeholder I needed. The only problem was that I couldn't figure out how to get to the scale I wanted without millions of dollars of VC funding (which I didn't have).*
>
> *At the time of launch, we powered a social gifting marketing campaign for Noel Gallagher's band High Flying Birds, which was seen by someone quite high up at Avon Cosmetics. She got in touch and asked if*

we could adapt what we'd built for her, as she wanted her customers to be able to send a product to a friend for free. When I visited, I was met by an incredibly successful woman who was really excited and told me that she'd be our first customer (and pay us) if we could do this for her. I had no idea what she was seeing but trusted that she was seeing something that I couldn't. Not knowing how to execute the original vision, I chose the path of least resistance and pivoted. It was only months later that I worked out what was so valuable about what Avon had asked for. That pivot changed the course of my business and was one of the best decisions I ever made.

Jonathan Grubin, *founder and CEO, SoPost*

Platform as a service (PaaS)

A category of cloud computing where developers are provided with an on-demand environment with the tools, infrastructure and operating systems for software development over the internet. SAP's cloud platform and Heroku are both examples of PaaS businesses.

Play to earn

This means that players can earn rewards and even money in the online games that they play. The play to earn movement is a rapidly emerging phenomenon in the world of gaming, where players of NFT games can swap or trade in-game NFTs with other players to earn profits.

Pre-emption rights (UK) / Pre-emptive rights (USA)

In the startup and VC world, these rights give existing investors the first chance to purchase new shares during future funding rounds, proportionate to their current ownership. This protects them from dilution (decreasing ownership percentage) when new investors come in.

Pre- and post-money valuation

When a company raises capital, investors can use pre- or post-money valuations of the company to denote the valuation of that business. A pre-money valuation is the valuation of the company before the value of the investment capital is added in. Post-money valuations include that investment capital value. For example, a post-money valuation of £5 million on a £1 million raise means the company had a £4 million pre-money valuation.

Preferred stock

Preferred stockholders have priority over a company's income and returns, so any dividends or proceeds from an exit are paid out before common stockholders receive their shares. Many investors will ask for preferred stock in their investment agreements at a post-seed stage, and convertible notes will frequently convert into preferred stock.

Pre-seed funding

The earliest stage of funding for a new company looking to get started, usually sourced from angels, family and friends (where applicable) and generally excluding any involvement from institutional investors, although there are an increasing number of micro-funds that are catering to pre-seed rounds.

Priced round

A funding round undertaken by a company where the price per share and valuation (or overall price of the company) is defined. This differs from convertible note rounds, where the valuation is formalised in a subsequent funding round.

Private equity (PE)

Investment funds, usually organised as limited partnerships, which buy and restructure companies. A private equity manager typically uses the money of its member investors to fund its acquisitions. Some examples of fund investors are hedge funds, pension funds and high-income individuals. PE funds usually operate at a later stage of the life cycle of a business, where the company has already raised multiple rounds of capital or achieved substantial profitability.

Product/market fit

A stage in a company's development where the product they have developed fits a clear need in the market. This is typically the stage at which the company starts to scale more rapidly, as reaching product/market fit implies that the product now solves a sufficiently large pain point that customers and/or users will be far more likely to download, engage with or purchase the product.

> *You have product/market fit (PMF) if 40+ per cent of your users would be 'very disappointed' if your service shut down tomorrow. Sean Ellis, who led growth at companies such as Dropbox and LogMeIn, arrived at this insight after years of trying to define what PMF looked like.*
>
> *Sean's test has become widely accepted by the startup and investor community as a great way to measure PMF. Another great way is to look for the 'Despite Moments'. Alex Weidauer, the founder and CEO of Rasa.ai (who raised $14 million in Series A from Accel and a Techstars Berlin alumnus), first introduced me to his Despite Moments idea a few years back when he was mentoring at Techstars.*
>
> *Alex knew that he and Alan Nichol (his co-founder) were on the right path with Rasa when he noticed that 'despite' not having a signup page, people would seek out their emails and contact them directly for early access. He noticed more and more Despite Moments where early adopters encountered friction or other barriers yet persevered despite the product not offering them an easy solution. Alex described these Despite Moments as magical early signals that they were on the right track.*
>
> *These are now what I look for as a founder and an early-stage investor. Other examples of Despite Moments might be seeing users*

- *hounding you for early access to a closed beta*
- *asking you how they can pay you when you have no payment pages*
- *start to hack your product for other use cases that you don't support (eg hashtags on X)*
- *spending a lot of time trying to get around a bug and sending you detailed bug reports*
- *being happy to attend long onboarding calls or fill out detailed questionnaires*
- *complaining about your product but continuing to use it*
- *spending time exporting and transforming their data into your format so that they can import it and play with your product.*

No founder wants to have Despite Moments (ie friction or gaps in their product), but don't forget the 'Alex Weidauer test' when it happens. Embrace these moments for what they are: early signals that you might be on the right path to PMF! If you have any other examples of Despite Moments, then I'd love to hear them. You can ping me on X @ConnorPM

Connor Murphy, *founder, Bridge*

Prompt engineering

A term that means crafting instructions, guidelines and examples for a large language model to help it perform a specific task. In the same way that software engineers program using code, prompt engineers program using language. For example, a simple prompt for an LLM might be: 'Write a children's story.' An engineered prompt would look something like: 'You are a bestselling children's author specialising in darkly humorous books. I want you to write a short bedtime story for a boy called Ned who is three years old. The story should contain references to his favourite toy, a green frog named Claude von Bibbett, who has a natty taste in scarves. It should also reference their love for cooking, bin trucks and football. The story should end with Ned falling asleep.'

Proof of concept (POC)

This term is generally used when B2B businesses begin to test their product and work with larger corporate or enterprise partners. A proof of concept at this stage is a testing phase where the startup can conduct a small test to determine the feasibility of a wider partnership or business relationship.

> *If your business relies on landing large customers, then step one is usually to get them to try the product. In most situations, depending on the size of the customer, the first step is usually to do a POC. The idea is to make sure that the customer gets to see value. We had to do this multiple times in the initial days, and still do. The hardest part is to make sure that you demonstrate real value without giving away the store.*
>
> *A POC should ideally be scope limited and budgeted, with clear metrics. You're not doing this as a freebie. Ideally you want the customer to agree about what success looks like as well as the next steps. The reason for this is to make sure that customers aren't merely kicking the tyres but are actually interested in buying the product! A great POC can immediately*

launch you into the right conversations. It's a phenomenal tool that we try to use as often as we can. In fact, we came up with an alternative approach by creating a demo site where the client can try our data product and the user experience for themselves and see a sample of the data instantly, with zero friction. We also created an analytics demo where the clients can explore the types of insights they can access with our services. The demos got rid of the need for a free POC, which was great. The POCs we do now are simply small-scale, paid pilots so we know that there's skin in the game on the client's side too.

Shruti Malani Krishnan, *founder and COO, PYInsights (Powr of You)*

Proof of stake (PoS)

A security mechanism for blockchains where only the people who own a specific cryptocurrency can validate transactions. It's a more energy-efficient way of validating transactions than proof of work, which relies on brute computing power.

Proof of work (PoW)

This is a blockchain consensus mechanism (see: Consensus mechanism) that involves utilising computing power to verify cryptocurrency transactions before they're added as a new block in the blockchain. Decentralised networks used by cryptocurrencies employ this consensus mechanism to ensure the integrity of the new data. PoW is a robust, proven way to ensure that a decentralised blockchain remains secure.

Proprietary

A term used to describe something that belongs to a startup, business or individual. Many machine-learning and AI companies have proprietary algorithms that they use to operate their business. This and other types of proprietary IP are highly valued by investors. Investors also frequently talk about proprietary deal flow, meaning unique access to certain deals.

Pro-rata rights

These are rights given to investors in a company to invest in future rounds of funding so that they can maintain their level of shareholding. It's a right rather than an obligation to invest. Many investors waive their pro rata. Others request super pro rata, where they're given the right to invest more and increase the size of their shareholding in subsequent rounds. However, this is far less common.

Public and private keys

These are the working parts of public key cryptography. Together, they encrypt and decrypt data that exists in a network. The public key can be shared widely while the private key should only be known by the owner. For example, public keys are like bank account numbers. They can be freely shared with everyone, and anyone can potentially send transactions to them. A private key is like a PIN, which, together with its corresponding public key information, grants you access to the actual funds in the account.

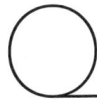

Quantum as a service (QAAS)

This is a cloud service that provides customers with access to quantum computing platforms over the internet. QaaS uses the SaaS commercial model, allowing customers to experiment with quantum computing on an on-demand basis with minimal financial output. An example of a QAAS service is Amazon Braket, which is a fully managed AWS service that helps developers, researchers and scientists get started with quantum computing. This can include building quantum applications and/or running algorithms on quantum computers.

Quantum computing

A next generation form of computing. Traditional computers use binary 'bits' representing a single binary value, typically 0 or 1, meaning it can only be in one of two possible states. A quantum computer uses 'qubits' that can both be on at the same time. This unlocks incredible computing power, meaning that information can be processed in a fraction of the time that the fastest binary systems can manage.

Ready, able, willing, impelled (RAWI)

A test that some founders use to decide whether they should start a business or expand their business into a new area. The premise is that you need to be ready, able, willing and impelled before you can make the right judgement about what to do.

Reality distortion field

This concept comes from an episode of *Star Trek* and is commonly used in the tech sector to describe how Apple co-founder Steve Jobs was able to convince others to achieve goals and complete tasks that were considered (by people other than Steve Jobs) to be impossible. More recently, it has been used to describe how WeWork's founder Adam Neumann and Elizabeth Holmes of Theranos were able to pull the wool over the eyes of investors, journalists and stakeholders alike. The most famous example of this came in an interview that *Forbes* writer Alex Konrad gave for Hulu's 2021 documentary *WeWork: Or the making and breaking of a $47 billion unicorn*. In it, he described how Neumann mixed up cappuccino and latte, leading to team members simply switching the meaning of each word. According to Konrad: 'It stood out to me as a strange, gratuitous reality distortion moment around Adam because he was ordering lattes but wanted cappuccinos. And rather than try to explain to him that he's wrong, they're just going to change the meaning of that word.'

Recapitalisation

Also known as a recap, this is where a company resets or cleans up its cap table. In this instance, previous investors are heavily or fully diluted to give the founders or new investors a larger share of the equity in the company.

Red and blue teaming

Teaming is a cybersecurity exercise that seeks to simulate a real-life cyberattack to help ascertain how well an organisation can withstand cyber threats. A red team serves as the attacker in this simulation, employing the same techniques as experienced hackers. A blue team defends and responds against the attack made by the red team.

Reinforcement learning

A type of machine learning where an agent learns how to behave in the best way in a given environment. Unlike so-called supervised learning, reinforcement learning doesn't rely on pre-labelled 'correct' answers. It explores, tests and works out the best actions to take based on feedback and its own experience. Perhaps one of the most famous examples of reinforcement learning is the computer program AlphaGo, which reached superhuman levels of ability while playing the board game Go.

Return on ad spend (ROAS)

A metric that's commonly used in marketing, especially online and mobile, to measure the efficiency of an advertising campaign by showing how much revenue is generated for every dollar spent on ads. Here's the formula: ROAS = (revenue attributable to ads / cost of ads). For example, if you spend £100 on an ad campaign and it generates £300 in sales directly attributable to those ads, your ROAS would be 3 (£300 / £100 = 3). If you want to express your ROAS as a percentage, multiply your result by 100.

Return on investment (ROI)

This is the ratio between net income and investment, and is habitually used as a sign of the efficiency or impact of investing capital.

Reverse vesting

This is where a startup employee earns most of their options towards the end of their vesting period. In a regular vesting schedule, employees vest over three to four years, with a one-year cliff, which means that they get the right to buy 25 per cent of their options at the end of the first year, with the remainder of their options vesting over the following 36 months. In the case of reverse vesting, employees vest smaller amounts in the first period of their employment, with a larger amount (equivalent to the cliff) vesting at the end of a three- to four-year period.

Right of first refusal (ROFR)

This allows an individual or business to conduct a business transaction before anyone else – for startups, ROFR offers remaining shareholders the right to purchase shares first, if any other shareholder chooses to sell them, before others can do so.

Roadmap

A long-term strategic document that details where your company or product is going, and the necessary major steps required to get there. A roadmap can also be a valuable communication tool for investors, as it helps to articulate strategic thinking behind the goal and the plan for getting there.

> Having a roadmap is a fundamental requirement for any startup or entrepreneur. A roadmap should be a high-level explanation of the future direction of the organisation and the development plans that ultimately ladder up to that business achieving its strategic goals. Potential investors will always be looking to understand the long-term plan to gauge the potential return on investment, while corporates assessing whether there's a valid partnership opportunity will want to understand if there will be sustained mutual benefits.
>
> When working for a pet insurance provider, I once assessed a partnership opportunity with a pet-tracking startup. My initial assessment of the technology revealed that their device wasn't providing the clinical-grade data that would make

them a valuable partner for me in the short term. They did, however, showcase an impressive roadmap that set out their company vision. It told the story of how their ambition wasn't just to be a pet tech business focused on the scaling of a single device, but how they wanted to build a whole ecosystem of solutions in the pet health space and eventually own the category. Seeing that development roadmap helped me to understand their vision and strategic direction. Later that year, we co-funded a research project, with the results benefiting both parties. Suffice to say that project wouldn't have gone ahead had that startup not communicated their roadmap and shown how we could learn together.

Jim Edwards, *digital innovation lead EMEA, Kimberly-Clark*

Rolling close

This is where funding comes in sporadically. Rather than pooling funding commitments together, they're spread out. This approach can damage FOMO (fear of missing out – your best fundraising asset to investors) and can disincentivise additional investors from getting involved.

Round

Also known as a fundraising round, this is what startups and investors call a qualified financing event, where one or more investors participate at the same time. For example, a startup may do a SEIS round of £150,000 from multiple investors. Once that money is wired and the legal documents associated with the round are signed, that round is deemed to be closed. The next time the company raises money, it triggers another round of funding. Many startups go through multiple rounds of funding: pre-seed, seed, A/B/C/D, bridge rounds, debt rounds and more.

Run rate

An estimate of a company's annual performance based on current data, usually from a shorter period such as a month or quarter. For example, if your company had £50,000 in revenue last month, your run rate would be £600,000. It's mainly used by founders when talking about fundraising. It can be a risky metric to use as it doesn't factor in things such as seasonality, which can impact a business over a 12-month period.

Runway

The amount of time a business can continue operating before it runs out of cash. This is generally a function of how much money a business has in its bank account and its monthly burn rate.

S

Scaleup

A stage in a company's growth cycle where it has achieved product/market fit and is scaling rapidly. The term is used to describe companies that, at a minimum, have raised at least a Series A, companies that have more than £1 million or $1 million in annual revenue. These businesses are usually seeing substantial growth in their user numbers, revenue, team sizes and more.

> A scaleup is a type of early-stage venture that has achieved significant growth in terms of revenue, employees, customers or market share. This is different from a startup, which is a new business that's still searching for its viable and scalable business model. A scaleup has already found its product/market fit and is focused on expanding its operations and increasing its impact. The term scaleup is regularly used in the context of innovation and technology, as these sectors tend to have high potential for rapid and exponential growth. However, they also exist in other industries as diverse as manufacturing, services or social enterprises. The main characteristic of a scaleup is that it has a proven and repeatable business model that can be applied to new markets, regions or sectors. Scaling up a business is not an easy task, as it involves many challenges and risks. Some of the common

challenges faced by scaleups are:

- *managing the increasing complexity and diversity of the organisation, such as hiring and retaining talent, developing a strong culture and establishing effective processes and systems that can be easily grown*
- *maintaining the quality and innovation of the product or service while meeting the growing demand and expectations of broader customers and stakeholders*
- *securing sufficient funding and resources to support the growth strategy, such as raising capital, managing cash flow and investing in infrastructure and equipment*
- *adapting to the evolving market conditions, competitor landscape and complying with new and changing regulations and standards.*

Finally, scaleups often drive solutions for solving social and environmental problems, as they naturally create positive impact through their innovative products, services and practices.

Mark Huxley, *founder of Huxley Advisory Limited and master, Company of Entrepreneurs*

Secondary selling

Where a company, individual or fund sells some or all of their ownership stake to another private investor prior to the company being publicly traded. Secondary sales usually happen in conjunction with funding rounds, allowing founders and early employees to sell some of their shareholding and get some liquidity.

The secondary market is where investors buy and sell securities they already own. A secondary transaction is when a new investor buys shares from an existing investor or investors. Secondary transactions or opportunities to sell the existing shares in startup companies mainly occur with new funding rounds. The new investor invests in new shares and buys some shares from the existing shareholder to secure a larger stake in the company. The price is often the same as in the funding round or slightly discounted. Recently, many secondary funds have been established that buy shares without new funding. The funds either find parties interested in selling their shares or are one counterparty in funding rounds but aim for the secondary shares only.

Due to the complexity of selling secondary shares, including tax structures, international law and other restrictions on the sale of shares, many marketplace businesses have started up to help solve these problems and make the process easier for all stakeholders. Some marketplaces provide matching between the seller and the buyer (eg ForgeGlobal), some build employee share trading (CartaX) and some run more complex trading pools (Funderbeam). In whichever form, a secondary share transaction is a great opportunity for founders, employees and early shareholders to get some liquidity (cash) before an unofficial exit (merger, acquisition or IPO).

Kaidi Ruusalepp, *founder and CEO, Funderbeam*

Securities and Exchange Commission (SEC)

A US government agency that exists to protect investors, support the fair operation of public and private markets and facilitate capital formation. Its remit covers everything from insider trading to crowdfunding, from public markets to startups.

Seed Enterprise Investment Scheme (SEIS)

This was launched in the UK to encourage investors to finance startups by providing tax breaks for backing projects they may otherwise have viewed as too risky.

> *This UK government tax initiative, together with its EIS big brother, fuels the early-stage UK startup scene. UK angel investors are able to claim a 50 per cent tax deduction (SEIS) or 30 per cent deduction (EIS) from that year's taxable income (lesser-known fact: they can also back-date the deduction to the previous tax year). If they keep their shares for three years, they pay no capital gains tax on a sale. And, if the company goes out of business, they can write off their investment. We estimate that 80 per cent of early stage (sub-£500k rounds) is SEIS/EIS investment. Frankly, it's a complete mystery why every other country hasn't copied the UK scheme (Ireland and Australia, among others, have had a go, but their schemes are rubbish and little used).*
>
> *The SEIS and EIS schemes have some seemingly*

odd rules, which on closer inspection are cleverly designed to close loopholes in previous HMRC investment schemes. For example, companies that are in oil or gas exploration or electricity generation can't offer SEIS/EIS tax breaks, likely due to the previous VCT investment scheme being exploited by funds setting up special-purpose vehicle energy companies and taking the tax benefits.

Some say that SEIS/EIS distorts the UK startup ecosystem ('Do you offer SEIS/EIS? Great, I'm in! Remind me again, what do you do?') and disadvantages companies that don't qualify (notably fintech/banking/leasing/energy). Founders of those companies definitely need to work harder to find investors, but that's minor compared to the huge amount of founder-friendly angel investor money available, which has produced an early-stage UK startup scene that's perhaps the most vibrant anywhere in the world.

Anthony Rose, *founder and CEO, SeedLegals*

Seed round

A funding round that usually involves large institutional investors. As of 2021, seed rounds in Europe are typically between £1 million and £3 million, with seed rounds in the US being between $1 million and $5 million. A seed round is generally also the first round in which an investor will require a board seat. Where pre-seed rounds are designed to help companies get the first version of their product to market, a seed round is about getting to product/market fit and preparing for scale.

In essence, the seed round marks the beginning of a startup's journey of seeking external investment and support to nurture their concept from a 'seed' of an idea into a metaphorical 'tree', and to fuel its growth. At this stage of fundraising, investors are usually angels or VCs, and sometimes strategic corporate investors. Amounts raised vary widely based on industry, startup size, investor involvement, etc. However, it's common for seed rounds in the UK to range from £250,000 to £2 million.

There are many important considerations to make and things to know before embarking on a seed round. Here are some that I think are of particular note, which I hope will be helpful.

Be aware of the language used and its meaning. Fortunately, you're reading this book, so you're already ahead of the game! Important terms include valuation cap (the maximum price per share that an investor will pay for company's shares), discount rate (the percentage off the valuation cap that investors will receive when they convert their debt into equity), term sheet, investor rights (any special rights or preferences given to the investors such as anti-dilution provisions, voting rights, participation rights in future funding rounds, etc), convertible note, capitalisation table, dilution and dilution protection.

Understand the different types of seed rounds – equity based, which involve the sale of equity in the company to the investors; and convertible note, which can be converted into equity at a later date – and which type best suits your circumstances.

The timing of a seed round is crucially important;

don't jump in too soon. A well-timed seed round often aligns with achieving significant milestones such as proof of concept, gaining traction in the market or demonstrating a viable product. Raising funds at this stage showcases your potential to investors, making the investment opportunity more compelling. At best, a poorly timed one lowers your valuation and at worst leaves you short of the funds needed.

Timing also affects a startup's runway – the length of time before it runs out of funds. A successful seed round at the right time ensures that your company has sufficient capital to sustain operations, achieve objectives and reach the next funding stage without running out of cash.

Don't waste funds raised. I've seen many examples of startups behaving like big corporates when receiving a cash injection. Treat it as if every penny is coming out of your own pocket. Cash is king!

Polish your pitch until it shines and find out what your investors are looking for before you turn up.

Judy Hadden, *female founder and past master, the Company of Entrepreneurs*

Semiconductor

A material whose electrical conductivity falls between that of a typical conductor (such as copper) and an insulator (such as glass). This controllable conductivity allows semiconductors to act as the building blocks of modern electronics. They form the basis for integrated circuits, transistors and diodes. They allow devices from pocket calculators to MRI machines to function. Semiconductors are often composed of elements such as silicon or germanium and have played a key part in the innovation of the tech industry over the past 40 years.

Series

Funding rounds are generally called Series X rounds: Series Seed-funding, Series A/B/C, and so on.

Series A

This is a round of funding of between $5 million and $30 million. Typically led by institutional investors or VC funds, a Series A is the first stage of growth funding that companies will receive. This is often the round where companies will start to spend larger amounts of money on marketing as they grow and scale.

Series B/C/D

These and subsequent rounds are usually referred to as growth capital, where the company uses the capital to increase their marketing spend, expand into new markets, acquire other businesses, expand their team and more. For the most part, these companies are already moving towards or are beyond profitability, and are preparing for an exit or IPO as the series moves through the alphabet.

Series C

A funding round that occurs when a company is well established and at the last stage of the growth cycle. This can be due to interest in scaling and expanding success or to address short-term challenges.

Series D

This funding is part of a company's growth capital. Larger venture capital and private equity funds usually participate in a Series D round. Funds generated are used to fuel growth, expansion, acquisitions and preparation for an exit or IPO.

Sidecar fund

See: Annex fund.

Sidechain

A separate, independent blockchain linked to a main blockchain (aka the parent or mainchain) using a two-way peg or bridge connection. This connection allows tokens or other digital assets to be transferred securely between the mainchain and the sidechain, allowing projects to expand their scale and ecosystem in a secure and decentralised manner.

Simple agreement for future equity (SAFE)

Similar to a convertible note, a SAFE is an investment agreement between an investor and a startup. The key difference is that a convertible note is a form of loan that attracts interest and has a maturity or conversion date. A SAFE has neither of those, which is why it's known as a 'simple' agreement. It's one of the most regularly used forms of investment at the early stage, particularly in the United States.

Small- or medium-sized enterprise (SME)

While many startups would be included in this category, SMEs don't always fall under the high-growth definition of a startup. Most SMEs don't have VC funding.

Smart contract

Computer code that automatically executes all or parts of an agreement and is stored on a blockchain-based platform. Unlike traditional contracts, smart contracts don't require the support of third parties or intermediaries.

Smoke testing

A software testing process that determines whether a deployed software build is stable. It consists of a minimal set of tests run on each build to test software functionalities. Smoke testing is also known as build verification testing or confidence testing.

Social web

Includes web-based services that enable community-based input and output, such as social networking websites Facebook and X (see: Web 2.0).

Software as a service (SaaS)

Cloud-based software that's owned, delivered and managed remotely by one or more providers, allowing users to subscribe to applications on a pay-as-you-go basis. Zoom, Shopify and Salesforce are examples of SaaS products.

> *When I first started using computers, buying software was like buying a cake: pay once and it's yours. You'd trundle home with a boxed floppy disk, CD or DVD. These physical tokens of the computing age granted you the right to use a specific piece of bugs-and-all software that would inevitably become outdated as soon as you installed it.*
>
> *As the screeching sound of dial-up tones heralded the 1990s, bulletin boards and the burgeoning web began to offer downloadable updates and signalled the end of the shiny disk era. The 2000s brought broadband and with it an epiphany in the software world: why settle for static software when it could evolve in real time, right alongside your growing collection of GIFs and dubiously acquired MP3s?*
>
> *Enter the age of software as a service (SaaS). In this brave new world, software wasn't just a product, it was a perpetual promise of improvement. For a monthly or annual fee, you'd get the latest features, updates and integrations, all served up through the cloud to your web browser or via continually updated apps on your mobile devices. No more installation, no more ownership, just seamless access on any device, anywhere – as long as you kept paying.*
>
> *As CDs and DVDs were relegated to being dangled on strings to scare birds, SaaS turned software into a constantly enhanced organism that grows, adapts and plays well with others. It also*

spawned a whole new language of metrics and money: ARPU, churn, MRR, ARR, CAC, and LTV became the new buzzwords of the startup world, the new totems of the SaaS faith, and opened up the market for a startup lexicon… but that's another story.

Adam Stamper, founder, xe.io

Spatial computing

See: Metaverse.

Split testing

See: A/B testing.

Stablecoin

A cryptocurrency whose value is tied to a stable asset such as the US dollar, gold or other fiat (government-issued) currencies. Think of it as a crypto-dollar.

Stage

Shorthand for the phase of development that a startup has reached. Pre-seed companies are usually at the idea/prototype stage, conducting customer discovery, initial pilots and tests, and iterating their idea. A later-stage company – Series A/B/C onwards – has generally reached product/market fit and is now rapidly scaling its business.

Startup

A new company or recently created business looking for a business model that's repeatable and scalable.

Static web

A collective term for websites that are delivered to every web browser and remain the same for every user (see: Web 1.0).

Stealth mode

How some founders describe their startup at its earliest stages. It's a term used by founders and teams to talk about how they're running their company without disclosing any information about the business, IP or other details that may be relevant to competitors. While it can be employed to protect an idea, it's also frequently used by founders to generate some buzz. The thinking behind this is that changing your job title on LinkedIn to 'founder at stealth startup' is a great way to attract investor attention.

Stochastic parrot

A term that's used as a critique of the limitations of some AI systems. In the same way that parrots mimic human speech but don't 'understand' the words, large language models generate coherent text but they're not reasoning or engaging in an actual dialogue.

Stock options

Also known as options, these are a benefit frequently given to early-stage startup employees or advisors, although some large companies such as Amazon, Facebook and others will give equivalent grants in the form of RSUs (restricted stock units). An option gives the grantee the

S

right to purchase those shares at a pre-agreed (typically low) price at some point in the future. Stock options are normally expressed in percentage terms or in terms of the number of shares being offered to an employee. Most stock options vest over a one- to four-year period, meaning that an employee earns the right to all of the stock options they've been offered over that period. Stock options are usually subject to a cliff (meaning that up to a year passes before you start vesting), have a strike price (the price per share that has been pre-agreed) and an exercise period (meaning that you have a limited time period to buy the stock at the agreed price after you leave a company). Option owners can have a substantial financial outcome in the event of working at a successful company where the share price increases substantially, while the option holder still has the right to buy shares at a far lower price and then sell them for a substantial profit. For example, early team members become million-aires (and in some cases, billionaires) when they sell their early options in the company after its IPO.

Sweat equity

When you give shares in your company to early employees or contractors in place of cash. It's a common practice in startups that haven't yet raised funds. If you take a chance with a startup, your shares might become lucrative when the company sells.

> *On paper, sweat equity is attractive to an early-stage business where funding is tight but their plans need to be accelerated. If a required service can be provided for equity rather than paid for from*

company funds, then surely it's a no-brainer?

The pitfall is that whoever is providing the service is typically doing so in their downtime, which means it isn't prioritised in the same way as paid work. Corners can be cut and timeframes not met because the service provider needs to earn a living or generate a profit. If possible, I'd suggest steering clear of sweat equity. Focus on fundraising and perhaps consider raising at a reduced valuation to generate enough funds to allow you to reach the next significant milestone. If that's not achievable, then use sweat equity as a fallback. If it becomes necessary, stay close to the sweat equity provider. Scrutinise their work early on and continue to scrutinise it. If you see a lack of quality, or deadlines start to be missed, then you should be concerned. Try to resolve any challenges early on and make sure you have some form of get-out agreement regarding quality and timings to allow you to walk away if you need to.

Howard Simms, *investor and co-founder, Apadmi*

Switching costs

The difficulty or costs (psychological, financial, effort and time based) that are incurred by switching from one product or service to another.

T

Tag-along and drag-along rights

Tag-along rights protect minority shareholders by allowing them to join a sale of shares if initiated by a majority shareholder(s). A drag-along right enables a majority shareholder to force minority shareholders to consent to the sale of a company.

TAM/SAM/SOM

These acronyms stand for total addressable market (TAM), serviceable available market (SAM) and serviceable obtainable market (SOM). They're frequently used together during fundraising to illustrate the market opportunity for a startup. One of the best-known examples of TAM/SAM/SOM is contained in Airbnb's 2008 pitch deck. In it, they estimated the TAM at two billion total trips booked worldwide, of which 560 million were budget and online bookings. They estimated they could capture 84 million total trips (15 per cent of the SAM). They then estimated the average revenue generated per trip as a way of showing the market opportunity they were targeting.

( )tech

There are many sub sectors of the technology industry using various different terms that are portmanteaus of the word tech preceded by the sector that company is working in or targeting. The best known of these is fintech. Companies in that sector include businesses such as Transferwise, Revolut, Cuvva, Monzo and many others, all companies that are innovating in, partnering with or disrupting established companies in the finance sector. There are several other examples, including cleantech (companies that are working towards a cleaner environment and substantial energy savings), climate tech (see separate entry), adtech (advertising), edtech (education) and insurtech (insurance), to name but a few.

Tech debt

Also known as code debt, this is a common term in software development, where developers delay features and functionality and/or settle for suboptimal performance to push the project forward. A 'build now, fix later' mentality.

Term sheet

A document outlining the terms and conditions of a potential business agreement, setting out the basis for future negotiations between the seller and the buyer. It's usually the first documented evidence of a possible investment or acquisition and can be binding or non-binding.

Ticket size

A term used by angel investors and venture capital funds to describe the size of investment cheque they write. For example, an angel investor might have a ticket size of £1,000 to £10,000. A pre-seed fund might have a ticket size of £250,000 to £5 million. Some late-stage investors also use a variation of this phrase to refer to their 'minimum ticket size', which means the smallest cheque or investment they can make into a company.

Tokenisation

Digital asset tokenisation is the process by which ownership rights of an asset are represented as digital tokens, which are then stored on a blockchain. Tokens are like digital certificates of ownership and can represent almost any object, including physical, digital, fungible and non-fungible assets.

Traction

A term used to measure a startup's progress and momentum. It shows how well the company is gaining customer interest, user engagement, market demand and revenue. Essentially, traction proves that the startup's products or services are resonating with their intended audience.

Tranches

When an investor commits to financing but doesn't offer all the money to a business all at once. Each portion, or tranche, is released only when the company hits agreed-upon targets.

Turing test

Named after the Second World War computer scientist Alan Turing, this is one of the oldest methods for assessing AI, dating back to the 1950s. In the test, a computer and a human are asked questions, and a judge has to determine which one is human based on their answers. If the computer is indistinguishable from the human, it ultimately passes the Turing test.

Two and twenty (2 and 20)

A commonly used venture capital fund compensation structure. The 2 per cent represents a standard management fee, which is applied to the total assets under management. The 20 per cent is a performance fee, which is charged on the profits that the fund generates. For example, a £100 million fund would collect £2 million per year during the investment period, with a reduced amount for the remainder of the fund life, typically 1 per cent. If that fund then generated a profit of £50 million, the fund would take a 20 per cent fee (£10 million) as the reward for a successful outcome.

Ultra high net worth individual (UHNWI)

To be a UHNWI, you need to have at least $30 million worth of net investable assets in your name. However, this is only a guide, as there's no standard legal threshold. As the name suggests, UHNWIs are the wealthiest people in the world.

Unicorn

A privately held startup company valued at more than $1 billion.

Unit economics

A way of measuring the profitability (or potential profitability) of a company. The unit economics are calculated by looking at the revenue and costs associated with your business. For example, in a SaaS business, each customer could be defined as a unit, so the calculation of the value of each unit is the lifetime value of that customer minus their customer acquisition cost. This is also referred to as contribution margin.

Up round

A round of financing in which the company's worth has gone up since its previous valuation.

Upstream integration

When a company begins to control more of the parts of their business. For example, a direct-to-consumer business might buy their own manufacturing equipment rather than outsourcing, or a SaaS company might build their own internal tools rather than using third-party ones.

V

Validated learning

This allows you to quantify and (dis)prove a hypothesis. If you conduct 50 user interviews about a new feature and 80 per cent of people say they wouldn't pay for it, that can be seen as a validated learning. Likewise, you can use split tests on your website to get validated learning about conversion rates and more.

Validators

A participant in a proof of stake blockchain network that's ultimately responsible for validating new transactions and thus upholding the security of the blockchain. This validation process involves checking that the blockchain transactions are valid and in accordance with the network's rules and also ensuring that the sender has enough funds to complete the transaction. In return for their work, validators will receive transaction fees.

Valuation

The current actual or theoretical worth of a company. Many methods are used to set a value to a company. In public markets, a company's valuation (or market cap) is determined by its share price. However, with private/ early-stage companies, this is far more difficult. In early rounds, valuation is typically determined using multiple data points, ranging from tangible ones such as growth, revenue or MAU/DAU, to intangible ones such as the amount of excitement or hype that surrounds a company or founding team.

> *Setting and agreeing a valuation is both an art and a science. It's also a critical component of any deal: unrealistic valuation expectations on the part of the entrepreneur and/or investors can sink it.*
>
> *It's important to remember the following:*
>
> *The valuation number will change as the startup moves from a seed round through to Series A, B and so on. For established companies, valuation is built on past data and projections. Startups will have little or no historical trading data for the first few rounds and must rely on projections. They'll be discovering all kinds of new quirks about the business but will be able to access increasing amounts of relevant data as they scale. Some quirks will be positive but there will also be setbacks. So, understand how what you're discovering may impact the valuation and plan to learn from what's happening in the business. Entrepreneurs and investors will often have very different views about the basis, reliability and reasonableness of projections. The more an entrepreneur can adduce factual data to support a projection, the more successful a pitch will be, and the greater confidence in a valuation too.*
>
> *There's no single mathematical formula for a valuation. It can be the most counterintuitive element of an investment round. If the valuation is too high, investors may be put off and the value will never be realised. Too low, and you've sold the entrepreneurs*

and previous investors short. A key question in the minds of investors and entrepreneurs here is: how much of a stake is being bought for how much investment? The valuation underpins this debate.

The main thing for an entrepreneur to remember is that investors are looking for a return on their investment in you – and that most likely is in the form of an exit. Put yourself in their shoes and understand what return they need to say yes. If you can show you can meet this requirement with a degree of confidence, you're more likely to succeed.

Examples of poor valuation reasoning include:

- The copycat error: 'I was at an event last week and a company that looks a bit like ours was valued at x so we're going with that.'
- The massive market error: 'We're pre-revenue but based on the size of the total available market and the large percentage of that market we plan to capture, the valuation is y.'
- The product uniqueness error: 'Our tech is unique and has no direct competitors. Customers will therefore be plentiful. We anticipate that several major multinationals will compete to buy us up.'

You have a better chance of getting an agreement between the parties by having a reasoned valuation in which you:

- provide as much solid evidence as possible – primary data is best
- have a solid baseline business plan: it will undoubtedly evolve but will show how you think about your business

- *have a thorough grasp of your risks, are open about them and how you propose to address them*
- *use several methods as inputs to your valuation proposal. It will usually be prudent to show a comparison of several common valuation calculations relevant to your industry and your company at its present stage, eg DCF, EBITDA, revenue growth and other metrics.*

It's important to look at a potential valuation using several methods because, as stated above, valuations are both an art and a science. And, until proven otherwise, they're a matter of opinion, not fact.

Lisl Macdonald FRSA, *ex BT, Virgin, Ogilvy; founder, Spring and Atlas; angel investor and NED*

Value proposition

A company's value proposition details the benefits and/ or economic value that it promises to deliver to existing and future customers. It's usually a part of a company's marketing strategy, helping to differentiate the brand in question and to establish its position in the marketplace. As well as a concise statement of key benefits, value propositions can also serve as a declaration of purpose and intent, both in the marketplace and within the company itself.

In the constantly changing marketplace of ideas and innovations, the concept of a value proposition stands as a beacon, guiding both entrepreneurs and established businesses toward the holy grail of customer connection. It's more than a statement of function; it's a declaration of purpose, a bridge built on the understanding that what we offer can transform our customers' world.

I always advise entrepreneurs that they're not just selling a product or service; they're offering a key to a lock. Their value proposition is the map that shows why their key, among a sea of contenders, fits perfectly. It's not solely about the features or the price point; it's about the story, the why, the heartbeat of their offering. This narrative is what resonates, compelling a customer to pause and think, 'Yes, this is exactly what I need.'

Through my startup mentoring sessions, I've observed a common mistake: the failure to iterate on the value proposition based on customer feedback. Entrepreneurs often fall in love with their initial idea and neglect to refine their offering as they learn more about their customers' needs and pain points. This lack of adaptability can be a major bottleneck for a startup's growth, necessitating a pivotal movement in the growth path when necessary.

Conversely, a best practice is embedding the value proposition into every aspect of the customer experience. Successful startups don't just articulate their value proposition at the point of sale; they ensure it's experienced at every touchpoint, from marketing materials to customer service. This holistic approach reinforces the value proposition, building a stronger, more loyal customer base.

Incorporating these insights can elevate a good

> *value proposition to a great one, making it not only a statement but also a living, breathing part of your business that continuously attracts and retains customers.*
>
> **Dr Eren Kocyigit**, *founder, NBT Digital*

Venture building

Venture builders (aka startup factories, startup studios, tech studios and venture production studios) are companies that build out new business ideas in conjunction with entrepreneurs and (in some cases) corporate partners. They typically fund the ideation and development phase of the business, using their own resources, talent and networks. In return, they take a significant ownership stake. Examples of established venture building companies are Founders Factory, Betaworks and Expa. Some successful companies that have emerged from startup studios include Giphy, Dollar Shave Club and Hims.

Venture capital (VC)

An asset class that's focused on investing in earlier-stage, illiquid assets such as startups. Venture capital is generally a higher-risk investment, as there's a substantial failure rate with early-stage businesses compared to publicly traded or other liquid assets. Venture capital is typically deployed via funds that pool capital from LPs and then have their team and partners invest in the companies on their behalf. VC funds can be generalist or sector/stage/geography specific.

Venture capital trust (VCT)

An investment vehicle that operates in the United Kingdom. The VCT is a closed-end fund that was created by the UK government in the 1990s to help drive direct investment into local private businesses. These funds are tax efficient and allow individual investors to access venture capital investments via capital markets. VCTs seek out potential venture capital investments in small, unlisted firms that are in their early stages to generate higher than average, risk-adjusted returns. VCTs are commonly listed on the London Stock Exchange (LSE).

Venture debt

A type of financing provided to startups by specialist lenders and banks. It's generally raised alongside an equity funding round and is used to cover working capital or capital expenditure for equipment, etc. The main difference between venture lending and more traditional bank loans is that venture debt providers typically work with companies that aren't cash flow positive or are at an earlier stage. Venture debt providers also take warrants to invest in companies and can end up owning substantial stakes if repayments aren't kept up.

Vertical

Used to describe a group of companies that focus on a shared niche. Many VC funds, accelerators or CVCs are vertical or sector-specific, with a focus on sectors such as fintech, healthtech and medtech (see: ()tech).

Vertical integration

When a company extends all operations to ensure that it's in control of the whole supply chain, from manufacturing to end sales.

Vesting

A legal term that means to give or earn the right to a present or future payment, stock, asset or benefit. In startup employee agreements, people are paid a combination of salary and stock options. Those options give employees the right to buy equity in the company at an agreed (often discounted) rate. In most cases, those options vest or accrue to the employee over a given period, usually three to four years.

Web 1.0

The first stage of the evolution of the internet. In the early days of the World Wide Web, there were only a few content creators. It was a one-to-many model, with the majority of people consuming. For the most part, Web 1.0 sites were static pages with little or no user interaction.

Web 2.0

Also known as the social web, this is the second stage of development of the internet, characterised by the transition from static web pages to dynamic or user-generated content. It heralded the rapid growth of social media and other services, which ran on the basis of gaining access to personal data for advertising purposes.

web3

This is the third evolution of the web, which has blockchain as its backbone, offering a governance layer for trusted transactions. It's built upon the core concepts of decentralisation, openness and greater user utility – a decentralised network without the need for third parties.

White label

This type of technology is a ready-made licensed software product developed by one company and then rebranded by another to appear as its own.

Z

Zero data retention (ZDR)

This means not intentionally storing any data after it has served its immediate purpose. Instead of saving it for any potential future use, the data will be deleted as soon as it's no longer required.

Zone of proximal development (ZPD)

This describes the space between what a learner can do without assistance and what they can do with guidance or in collaboration with more experienced peers. In the business world, ZPD can help with employee training and development, from delivering training materials to scheduling professional development opportunities. The original idea behind ZPD came from the Russian psychologist Lev Vygotsky in the early 1900s. Vygotsky believed that every individual has two stages of skill development: a level that can be achieved by themselves and a level that can be achieved with the help of outside experts.

Acknowledgements

I couldn't have completed the editions of this book without the help of many people. First and foremost, thanks to my wife, Katie, and my daughters, Charlotte and Annabel, for not only giving me the space but also having the patience to help me get through this process.

Thanks to the hundreds, if not thousands, of startups that I've met and spoken to over the past eight years. Without these conversations, this book would never have been written.

Thanks to Eamonn, for initially agreeing to meet for a coffee at very short notice, listening to my idea for this book and, without any fuss, agreeing to jump on board. A different response would've killed this idea for good.

Thanks to Paul and James at The Allotment brand design company for their superb front and back cover designs.

And finally, thanks to Sue, Bev, Andrew and Paul at The Right Book Company. Without their help and guidance, this project would never have crossed the line and would have remained a pipe dream.

Ken Valledy

Mum and Dad – thanks for the Spectrum and all the computers, internet connections, guitars, books, magazines and more. Far more than that, thank you for the support and love that allowed me to do the crazy things that led me to this point.

To Rachael and Ned – thank you for putting up with my hare-brained schemes, live-streamed dinners and associated mess in the kitchen, and the early starts, late nights and occasional moments of stress. You both find ways to amaze me and make me laugh every day, and I love you for that.

Thanks to all the founders, fellow mentors, colleagues, friends and acquaintances I've been lucky enough to work with, mentor and occasionally sing karaoke with as a founder, investor and more at Techstars, The Fund, Tera Ventures and beyond. You're a huge part of the inspiration behind this book, and also a source of inspiration for so many of the definitions.

Thanks to Sue, Bev, Andrew, Paul and everyone at The Right Book Company for helping us make this a reality. Sorry for the occasional moments of stress, but hopefully we were generally better behaved and prepared the second time around…

A very special thanks to Ken for coming out to the Angel for a coffee and a chat, and for sharing the idea for this book. Seeing it in print was one big reward, but having the excuse for regular visits to The Hanbury was equally as much fun!

Eamonn Carey

In addition, we would both like to thank everyone who took time out to contribute stories and testimonials: Emma Jones, Jim Edwards, Shameen Prashantham, Raph Crouan, Shruti Malani Krishnan, Daniel Glazer, Jonathan Grubin, Christina Richardson, Andrew Backs,

Amy French, Jim Kite, Howard Simms, Mick Doran, Vijay Solanki, Inga Driksne, Daniel Sawko, Jan McGinley, Scott Newton, Naomi Timperley, Barney Worfolk-Smith, Jill Rudnick, Volker Ballueder, Agata Bendik, Mark Huxley, Judy Hadden, Adam Stamper, Lisl Macdonald, Dr Eren Kocyigit,

Andrus Oks, Anthony Rose, Monty Munford, Ian Hathaway, Connor Murphy, Kaidi Ruusalepp, Tom Eisenmann, Nicola Burnside, Matthew Fitzpatrick, Serena Martin and Jenny Fielding.